Diane
From Carl & Linda
Christmas 2002

The Cook's Canvas

A Collection of Recipes

FROM

ST. JOHN'S MUSEUM OF ART
WILMINGTON, NC

Library of Congress Card Catalog Number: 96-70027

Cover and endsheets are a detail of:
Minnie Evans (1892-1987)
Untitled (three faces surrounded by floral design), 1967
Crayon, graphite, and paint on paper collaged on canvas board
Gift of Mr. & Mrs. Bruce B. Cameron

Illustrations by Gladys Faris
Photography by Melva Calder

Printed in the United States of America
by Atlantic Printing
Tabor City, North Carolina 28463

TABLE OF CONTENTS

The Cook's Canvas

Chairmen
Lelia Birrell
Hilda Cameron

Executive Committee
Robin Hackney
Betty Oliver
Dixey Smith
Jane Sullivan
Polly White

Chapter Chairmen

Appetizers & Soups
Randi Duch
Pam Gordon

Poultry
Ruth Brown
Betty Oliver

Meat & Condiments
Robin Hackney

Seafood
Aggie Henriksen
Frankie Trask

Vegetables
Phiney Rhinehart
Darby Harris

Desserts
Agnes Anthony
Robin Ward

Pasta, Grains & Rice
Joy Kalogeropoulos

Professional Chefs
Polly White

Committee Chairmen

Public Relations
Margee Herring
Frankie Trask

Distribution
Jane Goodhue
Kay Schaal

Illustrator
Gladys Faris

Editorial Committee
Ede Baldridge
Pam Jobin
Katherine Phillips
Katharine Sullivan

Secretary
Angela Romanek

Treasurer
Robin Hackney

Volunteer Placement
Jinger Lyon

ACKNOWLEDGMENTS

We wish we could say that the genesis of *The Cook's Canvas* was carefully and painstakingly planned. The truth of the matter is that we were trying, and failing miserably, to become great watercolorists in an art class in 1991 when, being hungry, we started talking about food and recipes. It then seemed logical that we compile a cookbook and sell it for the benefit of St. John's Museum of Art. Little did we know! Five years, hours beyond count, and dozens of sleepless nights later, our casual conversation has taken form and here it is.

We can't thank the members of *The Cook's Canvas* Committee adequately. The success of this book is due to their tireless energy, enthusiasm, and sense of humor at moments when we had lost ours. We would particularly like to thank the following: the Executive Committee who read and considered every recipe; the chairmen of the Public Relations and Distribution Committee whose ideas and promotions presented *The Cook's Canvas* to many markets; our Illustrator and Editorial Committee who were able to make this publication a beautifully precise book. We could not have stayed afloat without the organizational skills of our Secretary, Treasurer and Volunteer Placement Chair. In addition, we would like to thank the core of our committee— the 300 or more volunteers (see list, page 300-301) —who contributed recipes, tested and retested them, and who conducted fund raising events which were vital to the financial security of this project. We couldn't have published this book without you.

Our angel is Rusty Carter, whose faith in what we were trying to accomplish made the birth of *The Cook's Canvas* possible. It is his contribution through his company, Atlantic Printing, to publish *The Cook's Canvas* at cost which made the project possible. We would also like to thank Gary Walker, General Manager of Atlantic Printing, who eased us through the technical problems.

Our donors are the backbone of our endeavor. We thank them for their support and confidence in our project and the Museum.

We are particularly indebted to Ren Brown, Director, St. John's Museum of Art, for his unflagging support and wise counsel; Pam Jobin, Assistant Director, and the rest of the Museum staff who cheerfully undertook the endless chores that were sent their way. Thank you for your patience.

A very deep thanks to our loyal friends and family who are 20 pounds heavier, who put up with us and loved us in spite of how "testy" we often became.

Enjoy The Cook's Canvas!
>   Lelia Birrell and Hilda Cameron
>   Chairmen

SPONSORS

Anne K. Beatty

Mr. & Mrs. George Birrell

Bruce B. Cameron Foundation

Daniel D. & Elizabeth H. Cameron Foundation

Mr. & Mrs. Russell M. Carter

Theodore Hobbs

Mr. & Mrs. Robert B. Kline

Tabitha Hutaff McEachern

Mobil Foundation, Inc.

Mr. John Murchison

Mr. Wallace C. Murchison

Mrs. Katherine Phillips

Mr. & Mrs. Fred Stone

Maxwell Lide Stanback Foundation

Mrs. Dorothy R. Werk

Mr. & Mrs. Henry Weyerhaeuser

FOREWORD

The history of St. John's Museum of Art is closely tied to the artists and art devotees of North Carolina who had the vision and desire to establish an art museum for the benefit of the citizens of Wilmington and Southeastern North Carolina. In 1962 while seeking a space to exhibit local artists' work, these enthusiastic art lovers received the gift of St. John's Masonic Lodge Building, dating to 1804. This generous contribution was a donation of Henry McKoy in memory of his brother James. Today, this beautiful and historic building houses the Museum's small but distinctive permanent collection of American art and its definitive collection of 18th, 19th and 20th century North Carolina art.

The ranks of St. John's Museum of Art's volunteers swelled over the years as did their vision for the Museum. In 1979, the Hughes Gallery and the Cowan House Studio were added to the Museum complex. In 1985, a beautiful walled Sculpture Garden was added to the landscaped grounds uniting the buildings.

Just as the Museum owes its very existence to the diligent and farsighted volunteers who directed St. John's Museum of Art through its formative years, the Cookbook Committee with its ranks beyond three hundred have donated five years and tireless hours of creativity, enabling *The Cook's Canvas* to become a reality. Through-out the entire project, from its conception to the final proof, two undaunted individuals made this cookbook a reality, chairmen of *The Cook's Canvas*, Lelia Birrell and Hilda Cameron.

Last but ceratinly not least I would like to thank the Sponsors who contrib-uted to this project so generously. Their investment will multiply many fold through the sale of *The Cook's Canvas* which will benefit a variety of exhibitions and educa-tional programs at St. John's Museum of Art for years to come.

I hope you enjoy these exceptional recipes and the selection of North Carolina and American art in St. John's Museum of Art's collection chosen for *The Cook's Canvas*.

C. Reynolds Brown
Director
St. John's Museum of Art

St John's Lodge
Wilmington N. C.

Henry Bacon (1866~1924)
St. John's Lodge, Wilmington, N.C., 1877
Watercolor on paper
Gift of Elizabeth F. McKoy

Born in Wilmington, NC, Henry Bacon was the renowned
architect of the Lincoln Memorial in Washington, DC.

Appetizers & Soups

Mary Cassatt (1844~1926)
The Letter, 1891
Drypoint and aquatint on paper
Gift of Terese Thorne McLane in honor of
Samuel Hudson Hughes and Zelina Comegys Brunschwig

Mary Cassatt was the only American invited to exhibit
her work in Paris with the French Impressionists.

BLT DIP

YIELD:
Serves 8

NOTES:
Try this!
It sounds peculiar, but your guests will rave.
For an elegant party serve in cocktail pastry shells.

1 cup sour cream
1 cup mayonnaise
1 pound bacon, cooked and crumbled
1 tomato, chopped
Freshly ground pepper to taste

- Stir together sour cream and mayonnaise.

- Just before serving, mix in bacon, tomato and pepper.

- Serve with toast points or chips.

MARINATED VIDALIA ONIONS

YIELD:
Makes about 1 1/2 cups

NOTES:
These also perk up burgers and sandwiches.

6 Vidalia onions, thinly sliced
1 cup vinegar
1 cup sugar
1 cups water
1/2 cup mayonnaise (not low-fat)
1 teaspoon celery seed
1 teaspoon celery salt
Crackers

- Soak onions in vinegar, sugar and water for 2 - 4 hours, or overnight, in refrigerator.

- Drain well. Toss with mayonnaise, celery seed and celery salt.

- Serve with crackers.

ROASTED GARLIC DIP

YIELD:
Serves 4

NOTES:
A delicious subtle taste.
Heaven for garlic lovers!

4 heads of garlic, tops cut off
$^3/_4$ cup olive oil
1 teaspoon dried basil
6 oil-packed sun-dried tomatoes
French bread

- Place garlic in an oven-proof casserole. Pour in enough water to cover garlic half way.

- Add $^1/_4$ cup olive oil.

- Bake at 350° for one hour, or until soft.

- In a saucepan, heat $^1/_2$ cup olive oil, add basil and cook 2 minutes.

- Cut tomatoes in small pieces with kitchen shears and add to saucepan.

- Squeeze garlic pulp from skin and combine with tomato mixture.

- Serve in a fondue pot, keep warm and dip with French bread.

FLORENTINE DIP

YIELD:

1 ¾ cups

NOTES:

A colorful dipping sauce for broccoli, cauliflower, carrots, slivers of red and yellow peppers, etc.

Try surrounding serving plate with cold cooked shrimp for dipping.

For a different taste: Add 1 (14 ounce) can artichoke hearts, drained and chopped.

1	(10 ounce) package frozen chopped spinach
¼	cup chopped scallions
1	cup sour cream
½	cup parsley, minced
½	cup mayonnaise
1	tablespoon lemon juice
1	teaspoon fines herbes
1	teaspoon fresh dill (or ½ teaspoon dried dill)
	Salt and freshly ground pepper to taste
	Paprika

- Defrost spinach, drain and squeeze dry. (To defrost quickly, place unopened package of spinach on plate and cook on high in the microwave for 5 minutes. Let stand until completely defrosted, remove from package, drain and squeeze dry.)

- Place spinach in food processor.

- Add remaining ingredients except paprika and blend well.

- Cover and refrigerate.

- Dust with paprika. Serve with raw vegetables.

HOT CRAB AND ARTICHOKE DIP

YIELD:
Serves 10

NOTES:
Clean crab by carefully removing cartilage. Do not rinse.

Serve with toast points or crackers.

3   tablespoons vegetable oil
1   onion, finely chopped
1   clove garlic, minced
$^1/_2$ teaspoon dried thyme
2   tablespoons chopped fresh basil
3   tablespoons chopped fresh parsley
2   cups grated Monterey Jack cheese, divided
    Hot pepper sauce to taste
2   (13 ounce) cans artichoke hearts, drained and chopped
1   pound fresh backfin crab meat, cleaned (see notes)
$^1/_2$ cup bread crumbs

- Heat oil in frying pan and sauté onion and garlic until soft. Remove from heat.

- Add herbs, 1 $^1/_2$ cups cheese and a dash or two of hot pepper sauce.

- Stir artichoke hearts into onion mixture.

- Gently fold in crab meat.

- Pour into a greased casserole and sprinkle remaining cheese and bread crumbs on top.

- Bake in a 350° oven for about 25 minutes, or until set.

SMOKED FISH DIP

YIELD:
Serves 10

NOTES:
Many fishermen smoke their catch. This is a delectable way to showcase it.

1 pound smoked trout, blue fish or salmon
8 ounces cream cheese
$^1/_2$ cup sour cream (or mayonnaise)
3 sprigs fresh dill, chopped
1 tablespoon capers, rinsed and drained
Salt and freshly ground pepper to taste
Paprika
Minced parsley
Dill pickles, sliced in $^1/_2$ inch rounds

- Process fish, cream cheese, sour cream (or mayonnaise), dill, capers, salt and pepper in blender or food processor.
- Place in serving bowl, sprinkling with paprika and parsley.
- Serve with dill pickles and crackers.

TARAMOSALATA

YIELD:
About 1 $^1/_2$ cups

NOTES:
A Greek classic - easy to prepare and delicious as an appetizer.

8 slices white bread, trimmed of crusts
2 (4 ounce) jars black domestic caviar
1 $^1/_2$ cups extra virgin olive oil
2 cloves garlic, minced
3 tablespoons fresh lemon juice

- Wet bread with water, then squeeze out moisture (it should have the consistency of wet cotton).
- In blender, combine caviar and $^1/_4$ cup olive oil. Process until blended.
- Add bread, garlic and remaining olive oil alternately with lemon juice.
- Blend until thickened.
- Cover and refrigerate.
- Place in a bowl and serve with crusty bread, crackers, or vegetables.

HIT OF THE PARTY BRIE

YIELD:
Serves 24

NOTES:
This lives up to its name.

Can be made several days ahead and kept in refrigerator unbaked.

1 tablespoon olive oil
1 large onion, chopped
1 red pepper, seeded and chopped
$^1/_2$ pound mushrooms, sliced
2 (10 ounce) packages frozen chopped spinach, thawed and drained
1 pound brie, rind removed

- Preheat oven to 350°.
- In skillet over medium heat, sauté onion and red pepper in olive oil until onion is translucent.
- Add mushrooms and sauté until soft. Remove from heat.
- Squeeze spinach dry and add to skillet mixture.
- Place in oven-proof dish.
- Cut brie in $^1/_4$ inch slices and layer over spinach mixture.
- Bake 10 minutes or until cheese melts.
- *Or*: Microwave on high for 2 minutes or until cheese melts.
- Serve with crackers.

SHRIMP MOLD

YIELD:

Serves about 20

NOTES:

A real wow at a cocktail party. A pretty change from shrimp with cocktail sauce.

For a different presentation, pour mixture into a lightly oiled jelly roll pan instead of mold. Chill and cut into shapes with a canapé cutter. Serve on Melba toast rounds.

1 (10 $\frac{1}{2}$) ounce can tomato soup
2 (8 ounce) packages cream cheese, softened
2 envelopes unflavored gelatin, softened in $\frac{1}{4}$ cup cold water
$\frac{1}{2}$ cup mayonnaise
$\frac{3}{4}$ cup chopped celery
$\frac{1}{2}$ cup chopped green pepper
1 onion, finely chopped
1 teaspoon salt
$\frac{1}{2}$ teaspoon paprika
3 dashes hot pepper sauce
1 teaspoon Worcestershire sauce
2 teaspoons prepared horseradish
1 pound cooked shrimp, chopped
   Melba toast rounds

- Heat tomato soup and blend in cream cheese until smooth.

- Thoroughly stir in gelatin until dissolved. Remove from heat. Cool slightly.

- Add remaining ingredients.

- Pour into 1 $\frac{1}{2}$ quart oiled mold and chill until set.

- Unmold on crisp lettuce leaves. Serve with crackers.

CHEESE PEAR

8   ounces Monterey Jack cheese, grated
14   ounces sharp cheddar, grated
1   (8 ounce) package cream cheese, room temperature
4   ounces Roquefort cheese, room temperature
    Hot pepper sauce to taste
1   cup toasted pecans, chopped
2   cloves garlic, minced
    Paprika
    Cinnamon stick, cut in pieces

- Mix all ingredients except paprika and cinnamon.
- Divide into three parts and shape each like a pear.
- Smooth sides and dust with paprika.
- Make the pear stem with a piece of cinnamon.
- Refrigerate.
- Let set at room temperature for 30 minutes before serving.

CHUTNEY NUT SPREAD

10   ounces chutney
$^1/_2$ cup coconut, toasted
12   ounces cream cheese
$^1/_4$ cup golden raisins
3   tablespoons sour cream
1   tablespoon curry powder
1   cup salted nuts, coarsely chopped
9   slices bacon, crisply cooked and crumbled
$^1/_3$ cup chopped scallions

- Reserve 2 tablespoons chutney and same amount of coconut.
- Mix together remaining ingredients.
- Place on a serving dish, or form in a flat circle on a platter.
- Top with reserved chutney and coconut.
- Serve with crackers or toasted pita triangles.

IT'S NOT JUST PIMIENTO CHEESE

YIELD:
Serves 20

NOTES:
If using roasted peppers, they should be minced when added to cheese mixture.

1 pound sharp Cheddar cheese, grated
$^1/_2$ pound Monterey Jack cheese, grated
1 tablespoon chopped fresh parsley
1 tablespoon snipped fresh chives
$^1/_2$ teaspoon dill
$^1/_2$ teaspoon celery seed
6 slices crisp fried bacon, crumbled
$^3/_4$ cup mayonnaise
5 roasted red peppers, [or 1 (7 ounce) jar chopped pimientos, drained]
   Freshly ground pepper
   Cayenne pepper

- Combine cheeses well in mixer.

- Add herbs and bacon.

- Stir in mayonnaise and carefully add red peppers (or pimiento). If serving as a dip instead of a spread, add more mayonnaise. Season with pepper and cayenne to taste.

BAKED CHÈVRE MARINARA

YIELD:
Serves 20

NOTES:
If you are in a hurry use your favorite jarred marinara sauce or use your own recipe.
Can be assembled ahead and refrigerated until ready to heat.

1 French baguette, sliced $^1/_4$ inch thick
   Olive oil
3 cups marinara sauce
2 pounds mild goat cheese, divided into 4 equal-sized pieces
   Fresh basil, minced
   Fresh oregano, minced

- Preheat oven to 350°.

- Brush baguette slices with olive oil and toast until crisp.

- Pour marinara sauce into quiche dish.

- Place goat cheese on top.

- Bake until sauce is bubbly and cheese is slightly soft.

- Sprinkle fresh minced herbs over top.

- Serve with toasted baguettes.

APPLE WALNUT PATÉ

YIELD:
Serves 20

NOTES:
This is so unusual that it's worth the effort.

If you soak apple slices in orange juice, they won't turn brown.

4	tablespoons unsalted butter
3	large shallots, minced
2	cloves garlic, minced
1	medium onion, chopped
2	apples, peeled, cored and chopped
1	pound chicken livers
8	ounces hot sausage, casings removed
$1/4$	cup brandy
8	ounces cream cheese, room temperature
$1/2$	teaspoon salt
$1/2$	teaspoon tarragon
$1/8$	teaspoon thyme
$1/8$	teaspoon allspice
1	cup walnuts, finely chopped

- Oil mold, and line it with plastic wrap.
- Melt 3 tablespoons butter and sauté shallots, garlic and onions.
- Add apples and cook until soft. Remove from pan.
- Melt remaining butter and sauté livers and sausage until cooked.
- Pour brandy over meat and ignite. Allow to cool.
- Stir apple-onion mixture into meat and purée in food processor.
- Remove to bowl.
- Mix in cream cheese, seasonings and nuts.
- Put in mold and refrigerate until set.
- Unmold and serve with crackers or apple slices.

SWEDISH PECANS

YIELD:
4 cups

NOTES:
Prettily wrapped, these make wonderful Christmas gifts for friends.

1 egg white, beaten
1 tablespoon water
1 pound pecan halves
1 cup sugar
1 teaspoon salt
1 teaspoon cinnamon

- Mix together egg white, water and pecans.
- Place on baking sheet.
- Mix sugar, salt and cinnamon and sprinkle on top of pecans.
- Roast one hour at 250°, turning every 15 minutes.

SPICY PECANS

YIELD:
4 cups

2 tablespoons olive oil
1 teaspoon cumin
1 teaspoon cayenne pepper
1 tablespoon Worcestershire sauce
1 teaspoon garlic powder
1 teaspoon salt
1 pound pecan halves

- Combine all ingredients in a plastic bag and shake.
- Place pecans on baking sheet and roast at 250° for one hour, turning every 15 minutes.

CAYENNE GINGER WAFERS

1 cup white cheddar cheese, grated
4 ounces margarine, softened
4 ounces butter, softened
1 teaspoon salt
$1/4$ - $1/2$ teaspoon cayenne pepper
1 cup flour
2 tablespoons candied ginger (about 5 pieces), finely chopped

- Cream cheddar cheese, margarine, butter, salt and cayenne.

- Add flour and mix thoroughly.

- Roll into a ball and wrap ball in plastic wrap. Chill 30 minutes.

- Divide dough in half, then halve the half and keep dividing until there are approximately 30 small balls.

- Put one piece of ginger in each ball.

- Place each ball on ungreased cookie sheet, flattening with the palm of your hand. Wafers will not spread so they can be placed close together.

- Bake at 350° for 15 minutes.

- Remove from pan and place on cooling rack.

LEEK AND RED PEPPER TARTS

Yield:
Makes about 66 small tarts

Notes:
For best results, these should be made the day they are to be served.

Using large muffin tins, they are fabulous with ham or grilled meat for dinner.

6   cups chopped leeks, white part only
2   tablespoons olive oil
2   cups chopped onions
3   cups chopped red pepper
4   puff pastry sheets, thawed
3   large eggs, beaten lightly
1   cup cream
1   teaspoon thyme
$^1/_4$ cup freshly grated Parmesan cheese
    Salt and freshly ground pepper to taste
    Small muffin tins

- Thoroughly wash leeks to remove all dirt.

- Heat oil in a large skillet or Dutch oven.

- Add leeks, onions and red peppers. Sauté until soft. Remove from heat and cool.

- Grease muffin tins. Cut pastry into squares larger than the cup. Place pastry over the cup and push down to line tin, using fingers.

- Mix eggs, cream, thyme and Parmesan cheese with the onion mixture. Add salt and pepper to taste.

- Fill each muffin cup half full of onion mixture.

- Bake at 350° for 20 - 25 minutes.

- Remove muffins from tins and cool on cooling rack.

SPINACH FRITTERS

YIELD:

Makes about 85 cocktail fritters

NOTES:

These freeze beautifully, and can be thawed and crisped in a 400° oven for about 10 minutes on an ungreased cookie sheet.

These can be a lovely addition to dinner. Measure batter by ¼ cups for dinner size fritters.

1   (10 ounce) package frozen chopped spinach, cooked and well drained
1   tablespoon butter
½   pound mushrooms, chopped
2   cloves garlic, minced
1   bunch scallions, with 2 inches of green stems, chopped
2   cups all-purpose flour
1   teaspoon salt
½   teaspoon sugar
    Freshly ground pepper
1 ½ cups milk
3   eggs
    Olive oil
    Canola oil
    Sour cream
    Red caviar

- Melt butter in a skillet; sauté mushrooms, garlic, and scallions until soft.

- Sift together flour, salt, sugar and pepper.

- In a mixing bowl, combine milk and eggs. Add dry ingredients and mix until just blended.

- Stir in mushrooms, garlic, scallions and drained spinach. Blend, but don't over mix.

- In a large heavy skillet, pour in half olive and half canola oils to a depth of ¼ inch, and heat.

- Drop in spinach mixture one tablespoon at a time and brown on both sides.

- Drain well on paper towels.

- Serve with a dollop of sour cream topped with red caviar.

CURRIED PUMPKIN MOUSSE

YIELD:

Makes about 48 appetizers

NOTES:

This unusual appetizer may also be served on raw zucchini rounds.

If you don't own a pastry bag for piping (or don't enjoy cleaning it), the zip-lock bag works beautifully.

2   tablespoons butter
$1/4$ cup chopped shallots
3   teaspoons curry powder
$1/2$ teaspoon cumin
$1/2$ teaspoon salt
    Freshly ground pepper
2   cups canned solid pack pumpkin
8   ounces cream cheese, softened
4   heads Belgian endive lettuce
$1/2$ cup chopped walnuts, toasted

- In a small saucepan, melt butter and sauté shallots until tender. Add curry powder, cumin, salt and pepper to taste.

- Cook, stirring, for one minute.

- In a food processor purée pumpkin and cream cheese. Add shallot mixture and blend.

- Transfer to a bowl or spoon into a gallon-size heavy-duty plastic zip-lock bag, and chill for at least 3 hours or overnight.

- When ready to serve, trim and separate endive leaves.

- Use a pastry bag fitted with a fluted tip or cut a small hole in one corner of a plastic bag.

- Pipe about 1 tablespoon of pumpkin on each leaf, and top with walnuts.

FIESTA POPS

YIELDS:
44 pitas

NOTES:
A joy to have on hand in the freezer!

2   packages pita pops (mini pitas - 22 in package)
1   cup finely chopped green onions, including green tops
1 ½   cups finely chopped black and green olives
1   teaspoon black pepper
1   cup mayonnaise
3   cups Monterey Jack cheese with jalapeño, grated

- With a sharp knife, cut slits into each pop.
- Mix remaining ingredients and stuff into pitas.
- Place on cookie sheet and freeze until hard.
- Store in plastic freezer bags until needed.
- Bake frozen in 350° oven for 10 to 15 minutes. Watch carefully; cheese runs.

TAMPICO GUACAMOLE

YIELDS:
about 1 cup

NOTES:
This, made with cottage cheese, is the original guacamole. It's still a favorite.

1   ripe avocado
¼   cup sour cream
¼   cup milk, *or*
½   cup small curd cottage cheese, instead of sour cream and milk
1   teaspoon minced onion
1   clove garlic, mashed with 1/2 teaspoon salt
1   tablespoon fresh cilantro, minced
½   teaspoon hot pepper sauce or more to taste
3   tablespoons lemon juice

- Peel avocado and mash with a fork to a smooth pulp.
- Add sour cream and milk (or cottage cheese), onion, garlic, cilantro, pepper sauce and lemon juice.
- Blend well with whisk or fork.
- Cover and refrigerate at least one hour before serving.
- Serve with tortilla chips and your favorite salsa.

MUSHROOMS IN CROUSTADES

YIELD:
Makes 48

Notes:
Toast croustades until golden brown and fill with Chicken Mango Salad (see page 182) or Marinated Vidalia Onions (see page 3).

4   ounces dried mushrooms
6   tablespoons butter
6   shallots, chopped
1   pound fresh mushrooms, chopped
$^1/_2$ pound Cremini mushrooms, chopped
3   ounces cream cheese
8   ounces ricotta cheese
$^1/_4$ cup sherry
1   tablespoon fresh tarragon chopped, or 1 teaspoon dried

- Soak dried mushrooms in hot water for 15 minutes, remove with a slotted spoon and chop.

- Sauté shallots in butter.

- Mix mushrooms, shallots and remaining ingredients and place in browned croustades.

- Bake at 350° for about 10 minutes.

CROUSTADES:
Butter to grease small muffin pans
Thinly sliced bread

- Brush melted butter in muffin pans.

- Using biscuit cutter or rim of drinking glass, cut out circle in slice of bread.

- Force bread into pan and bake at 300° until lightly browned.

BACON THROUGH THE RYE

YIELD:
Serves 8

NOTES:
Try making grilled mini-sandwiches!

$^{1}/_{2}$ pound sliced bacon, crisply cooked and crumbled
1   cup shredded Cheddar cheese
4   green onions, chopped
3   tablespoons mayonnaise
20   slices cocktail-size rye bread

- Mix bacon, cheese, onions and mayonnaise.
- Spread on rye slices.
- Broil until bubbly (about 2 minutes).

TORTILLA ROLL-UPS

YIELD:
About 5 dozen

NOTES:
For a Mexican menu, serve with our Tampico Guacamole (see page 18) and Green Enchiladas (see page 86).

8   ounces cream cheese
8   ounces sour cream
5   green onions, chopped
3   fresh jalapeños, seeded and finely chopped (wear rubber gloves), *or* 1 (4 ounce) can chopped green chilies for milder version
$^{1}/_{2}$ cup shredded sharp Cheddar cheese
2   tablespoons chopped black olives
   Lime juice to taste
   Garlic powder to taste
   Salt to taste
12   large flour tortillas

- Mix all ingredients (except tortillas) in food processor.
- Blend until smooth.
- Spread mixture on flour tortillas and roll up.
- Place filled tortillas seam side down on cookie sheet. Cover with damp paper towels.
- Chill until cream cheese is set.
- Cut tortillas into one-inch pieces and serve with toothpicks and your favorite picante sauce as a dip.

SPINACH STUFFED MUSHROOMS

YIELD:
Serves 10

NOTES:
Mushroom stems will freeze nicely in plastic freezer bags. Use for stock, gravy or soup.

For a variation, stuff mushrooms with Boursin instead of spinach.

24 large mushrooms
1 (12 ounce) package frozen spinach soufflé, defrosted
Freshly grated Parmesan cheese

- Remove mushroom stems.
- Wipe caps with a damp cloth. Do not wash.
- Place enough spinach in each cap to half fill it.
- Sprinkle with grated Parmesan cheese.
- Put on an oiled baking sheet and bake at 300° for 30 minutes, or until soufflé is set.

BOURSIN

YIELD:
Makes 24 ounces

NOTES:
This is delicious for stuffing mushroom caps, spreading on toasted baguette slices, topping tomatoes before broiling, etc.

2 (8 ounce) packages cream cheese, softened
8 ounces whipped butter
$1/2$ teaspoon oregano
$1/2$ teaspoon basil
$1/2$ teaspoon thyme
$1/2$ teaspoon marjoram
1 teaspoon cracked black pepper, or more to taste
2 cloves garlic, minced

- Combine all ingredients.
- Cover and refrigerate.

HOT AND SPICY SHRIMP COCKTAIL

YIELD:
Serves 4

NOTES:
The shrimp recipe can easily be doubled or tripled.

Boiling shrimp in water with one tablespoon of oil makes them easier to peel.

1   quart water
1   tablespoon salt
1   tablespoon coriander
1   tablespoon fennel seed
2   bay leaves
2   teaspoons to 2 tablespoons red pepper flakes, depending on taste
$1/4$ cup red or white vinegar
1   pound heads off raw shrimp
    Spicy Shrimp Sauce (see below)

- In a large pot, bring water, spices and vinegar to a boil.
- Add shrimp, and leave in water only 2 minutes or until light pink.

   Do not overcook.

- Drain shrimp and cool in a bowl or on a plate.
- Peel and serve with Spicy Shrimp Sauce.

SPICY SHRIMP SAUCE

YIELD:
Serves 4

NOTES:
Try the Spicy Shrimp Sauce spread on a toasted baguette, top with a shrimp and dill sprig, or over cold asparagus.

1   cup mayonnaise
    Juice of one orange
    Juice of one lemon
3   tablespoons ketchup
$1/2$ teaspoon cayenne pepper
1   clove garlic, minced
3   tablespoons prepared horseradish
1   tablespoon cognac

- Mix mayonnaise and juices.
- Add ketchup and cayenne.
- Stir in garlic, horseradish and cognac.

DILLED HAM BISCUITS

YIELD:

Makes 5 dozen

NOTES:

If you omit the dill, you have a great recipe for plain Ham Biscuits.

$^1/_2$ pound country ham, very thinly sliced
4 ounces chutney

BISCUITS:

2 cups all-purpose flour
2 teaspoons baking powder
1 teaspoon salt
6 tablespoons solid vegetable shortening, butter or margarine
$^2/_3$ cup buttermilk
1 tablespoon dried dill

- Preheat oven to 450°.
- Grease baking sheet.
- Sift flour, baking powder and salt into a large bowl.
- Cut in shortening.
- Add buttermilk and dill, blending thoroughly.
- Turn dough onto floured surface. Knead lightly for 1 minute.
- Roll dough to thickness of $^1/_4$-inch. Fold over, roll lightly with rolling pin so dough is $^1/_2$ inch thick.
- Cut into 1-inch rounds.
- Transfer to baking sheet.
- Bake until lightly browned, approximately 10-12 minutes.
- When biscuits are done and cool enough to touch, split and insert sliver of ham and a dot of chutney.

SKEWERED STEAK

YIELD:

Makes about 30 skewers

NOTES:

Guests have been known to follow the server into the kitchen for more!

2 pounds London broil steak
30 long bamboo skewers

MARINADE:

2 cups soy sauce
1/2 cup olive oil
2 tablespoons honey
2 tablespoons minced fresh ginger
2 tablespoons dry mustard
6 cloves garlic, minced

- Thinly slice London broil across the grain (meat is easiest to slice when it has been partially frozen).

- Combine all marinade ingredients.

- Coat each slice of meat with marinade, cover and refrigerate at least 4 hours, but preferably overnight.

- When ready to serve soak bamboo skewers in warm water for 30 minutes to prevent burning.

- Preheat broiler.

- Thread beef strips onto damp skewers.

- Arrange skewers so that ends extend beyond edge of broiler rack to keep them clean.

- Broil 1 1/2 minutes and remove from heat.

- Turn skewers over and brush the other side with marinade.

- Return to broiler and cook another 1 1/2 minutes.

- Arrange in a spiral pattern on a round platter.

- Serve hot or at room temperature.

RAJA CHICKEN BALLS

YIELD:
Makes about 30 chicken balls

NOTES:
Most unusual and very popular at parties.

4   ounces cream cheese, softened
2   tablespoons mayonnaise
1   cup chopped pecans
1   cup cooked finely chopped chicken
1   tablespoon chutney, chopped
1   teaspoon curry powder, or more to taste
1   cup grated coconut, unsweetened
     Cucumber Dip (see below)

- Mix all ingredients except coconut.
- Make into small balls and then roll in coconut.
- Chill until ready to serve.
- Serve with toothpicks and Cucumber Dip.

CUCUMBER DIP

YIELD:
3 cups

NOTES:
Cucumber Dip (Raita) is a traditional accompaniment for spicy Indian curries.

3   medium sized cucumbers, peeled
2   cloves garlic, peeled
3   green onions, chopped
     Salt and freshly ground pepper
1   tablespoon vinegar
1   tablespoon parsley
$1/4$ teaspoon ground cumin
1   cup plain yogurt

- Place all ingredients except yogurt in food processor.
- Pulse until finely chopped.
- Add yogurt and process briefly to blend.
- Serve chilled.

MELON SOUP

YIELD:
Serves 4 - 6, depending on size of melons.

NOTES:
This beautiful dish, pink and pale green, is a delight on a hot summer evening.

1 ripe cantaloupe, seeded
1 ripe honeydew, seeded
2 tablespoons lemon juice
2 tablespoons lime juice
  Mint sprigs for garnish

- Scoop seedless pulp from cantaloupe and purée in blender or food processor with lemon juice. Place in large pourable container.

- Rinse out blender or food processor and repeat process with honeydew and lime juice. Place in another pourable container.

- Chill both containers several hours.

- To serve, simultaneously pour the two purées into individual chilled soup bowls, keeping the colors distinct. Garnish with mint leaves.

COLD BLACK BEAN SOUP

YIELD:
Serves 6 - 8

NOTES:
For color add any or all of the following: chopped green peppers, diced tomatoes or lemon slices.

2 (16 ounce) cans black beans, not drained
$1/2$ small onion
4 ounces hot salsa
16 ounces non-fat yogurt
8 fresh cilantro leaves
1 (14 $1/2$ ounce) can chicken broth
  Salt and pepper to taste
  Sour cream as garnish

- Place all but chicken broth in food processor or blender and blend until completely smooth.

- Pour into saucepan. Add broth, and bring to a simmer.

- Remove from heat and serve either at room temperature or chilled.

- Serve with a dollop of sour cream and tortilla chips.

CHILLED FRESH TOMATO SOUP

YIELD:

Serves 8 - 12

NOTES:

When making croutons use oregano, basil, garlic, salt and freshly ground pepper. These herbs and spices will complement the tomato flavor.

12 large ripe tomatoes
2 small onions, grated
2 teaspoons salt
2 teaspoons black pepper
1 tablespoon sugar
1 tablespoon fresh basil, minced, (or 1 tablespoon cilantro, chopped)
1 fresh jalapeño pepper, seeded and minced (wear rubber gloves)
   Sour cream or plain yogurt

- Peel tomatoes by immersing in boiling water for 20 seconds. Lift from water, cut out core and peel away skin.

- Mash them thoroughly with a potato masher in a large bowl.

- Add onions and stir in salt, pepper, sugar, basil (or cilantro) and jalapeño.

- Chill several hours or overnight.

- Adjust seasonings, and serve in bowls with a dollop of sour cream or yogurt.

- Sprinkle croutons on top.

CROUTONS:

1 loaf French bread
   Olive oil or butter
   Herbs
   Salt
   Freshly ground pepper

- Cube French bread.
- Heat olive oil or butter with your choice of dry herbs, salt and pepper.
- Toss with cubed bread.
- Spread in single layer on jelly roll pan.
- Bake at 250° until lightly browned, stirring occasionally.

CREAM OF CUCUMBER SOUP

YIELD:
Serves 8

NOTES:
Refreshing for a summer evening.
This will cause delight rather than panic when cukes have taken over your garden.

2   medium yellow onions, sliced
3   tablespoons butter
3   eight-inch cucumbers, peeled and sliced
6   cups chicken broth
2   tablespoons tarragon vinegar
1   tablespoon fresh tarragon
4   tablespoons quick cooking farina (cream of wheat)
    Seasoned salt
    White pepper
1 ½   cups sour cream
1   tablespoon tarragon

- Cook onions slowly in butter until tender but not browned.
- Add cucumbers, chicken broth, vinegar and tarragon.
- Bring to a boil, then stir in farina.
- Boil for a minute to cook farina, then reduce heat to simmer for 25 minutes.
- Purée in a blender and strain into a large bowl.
- Add seasoned salt and white pepper to taste.
- Add several tablespoonfuls to one cup sour cream and blend. Fold into remaining cucumber mixture.
- Chill for several hours.
- Serve with a dollop of sour cream and tarragon sprinkled on top.

ARGYLE GREEN PEPPER SOUP

YIELD:

Serves 4

NOTES:

This is equally good made with red, yellow, or orange bell peppers.

It is important to strain after processing to remove bits of skin.

May be served hot or cold.

2 tablespoons butter
2 tablespoons olive oil
2 large green bell peppers, seeded and diced
2 medium onions, chopped
1 1/2 tablespoons flour
1 1/2 cups chicken stock
1 1/2 cups milk
Salt and freshly ground pepper
Heavy cream for garnish

- Heat the butter and oil in a saucepan.
- Add the peppers and onions and simmer, stirring occasionally, for about five minutes.
- Stir in the flour and cook for one minute.
- Blend in the stock and bring to a boil, stirring until thickened.
- Season with salt and pepper, then cover and simmer for 10 minutes, or until vegetables are tender.
- Purée the soup in a food processor.
- Strain contents back into the pan and add the milk.
- Stir while bringing gently to the boil.
- Adjust seasonings and serve in bowls.
- Garnish with a swirl of heavy cream.

BUTTERNUT SQUASH SOUP

YIELD:

Serves 6

NOTES:

This can be a year-round soup.

If it is to be served cold, use 8 ounces of plain yogurt, to which several drops of hot pepper sauce have been added, instead of jalapeño cheese.

4   cups chicken broth
1   tart apple, cored, peeled and quartered
1 1/4   pounds butternut squash, peeled, seeded and chopped
3   tablespoons raw rice
1   medium onion, chopped
1   teaspoon sugar
1/4   teaspoon curry powder
1/4   cup heavy cream
6   ounces Monterey Jack jalapeño cheese, cubed
  Salt and freshly ground pepper to taste
  Milk to stretch, if necessary

- In a large saucepan, simmer broth, apple, squash, rice, onion, sugar and curry for 35 - 45 minutes. Cool slightly.
- Purée in blender or food processor and return to pan.
- When ready to serve, reheat, adding cream, cheese, salt and pepper.
- Stir until cheese is melted.
- If soup is too thick, add milk to reach desired consistency.

ZUCCHINI AND ROSEMARY SOUP

YIELD:
Serves 4

NOTES:
The flavor of rosemary makes this distinctive.

4 tablespoons butter
2 medium onions, chopped
1 ½ pounds zucchini, sliced
1 clove garlic, skinned and crushed
2 teaspoons fresh rosemary leaves
1 ½ cups chicken broth
Salt and freshly ground pepper to taste
Plain yogurt to garnish

- Melt butter in medium pan and add onions.
- Sauté for about five minutes, stirring occasionally.
- Add sliced zucchini and continue cooking five more minutes.
- Add garlic, rosemary, broth, salt and pepper.
- Simmer, covered, for 25 minutes.
- Cool slightly and process in blender or food processor, in batches if necessary, until smooth.
- Serve hot. Garnish with yogurt.

SOUPER SPINACH

YIELD:
Serves 6

NOTES:
This lovely soup must be made with fresh spinach.

3   pounds spinach, thoroughly washed and stems removed
4   ounces butter
1 ½   cups chopped onions
2   cloves garlic, minced
2   cups chicken broth
2   cups whole milk
1   teaspoon salt
½   teaspoon hot ground black pepper
¼   teaspoon hot pepper sauce
2   tablespoons fresh lemon juice
2   tablespoons heavy cream
    Freshly ground nutmeg

- With only the water left on spinach after washing, cook over low heat in a large pot until leaves are wilted and reduced.

- Drain the spinach, reserving the liquid.

- Melt butter and sauté onions and garlic.

- In a food processor, purée spinach, onion and garlic until very smooth.

- Combine purée in large pot with the reserved spinach liquid, chicken broth, milk, seasonings and lemon juice (if spinach is very hot, mix a little milk in it first to prevent curdling).

- Stir in cream and simmer five minutes. Serve warm or cold, sprinkled with nutmeg.

GARLIC SOUP

YIELD:
Serves 4

NOTES:
This delectable soup may be made a day ahead.

It can be doubled.

Don't be intimidated by the large amount of garlic. Garlic takes on a very mild, sweet flavor when roasted or cooked for a long period of time.

A quick way to peel garlic: Place cloves on a cutting board and smash with flat side of a chef's knife.

1	tablespoon butter
1	tablespoon olive oil
1	pound onions, coarsely chopped
28	medium garlic cloves, peeled (about 2 heads)
3	cups chicken stock
1 $^1/_2$	cups French bread, cut in $^1/_4$ inch cubes
	Bouquet garni (5 parsley sprigs, 3 thyme sprigs, $^1/_2$ bay leaf - tied in cheesecloth for easy removal)
1	cup whipping cream (or half and half)
	Salt and freshly ground pepper to taste

- Melt butter and oil in large heavy skillet or Dutch oven over low heat.

- Add onions and garlic. Cook over low heat, stirring frequently, until tender and golden (approximately 30 minutes).

- Add stock, bread and bouquet garni and bring to a boil.

- Reduce heat and simmer 15 minutes.

- Remove bouquet garni.

- Purée mixture in blender or food processor, in batches if necessary.

- Pour purée into heavy saucepan and mix in cream.

- Stir over low heat until thoroughly heated.

- Add salt and pepper to taste.

PECAN SOUP

YIELD:
Serves 6

NOTES:
Soup should be smooth, but with the crunch of pecans throughout.

3 tablespoons butter
1 medium onion, chopped
$^1/_2$ cup chopped celery
3 cups chicken broth
1 $^1/_2$ cups chopped pecans
1 cup chopped carrots
2 tablespoons minced parsley
1 teaspoon poultry seasoning
$^1/_2$ teaspoon salt
$^1/_2$ teaspoon dried basil, crushed
$^1/_8$ teaspoon cayenne pepper
$^1/_2$ cup heavy cream (or half and half)
$^1/_4$ cup cream sherry
Sour cream and chopped chives for garnish

- Melt butter in saucepan and sauté onions and celery until soft.

- Stir remaining ingredients except cream and sherry into onion mixture and simmer, covered, for 20 minutes.

- Process in blender until smooth, but still maintaining bits of pecans.

- The recipe, up to this point, can be prepared ahead of time and refrigerated.

- Return soup to room temperature.

- Blend in cream and sherry and heat through, stirring. Do *not* boil.

- Serve in bowls and top with a spoonful of sour cream sprinkled with chives.

CRAB BISQUE

YIELD:

Serves 6

NOTES:

*This beautifully rich
soup must be carefully
watched to keep it
from boiling.*

*It is a complete meal
with good, crusty
French bread and a
salad.*

6   scallions, finely chopped

4   tablespoons unsalted butter, cut into small pieces

$1/4$ cup flour

3   cups milk

$1 1/2$ cups heavy cream

$1/2$ teaspoon mace

$1/2$ teaspoon paprika

2   teaspoons salt

Hot pepper sauce to taste

1   pound lump or backfin crab meat, cleaned (see Notes, page 6)

Juice of one lemon

Fresh dill for garnish

- In a large stock pot sauté scallions in melted butter until soft.

- Blend in flour and cook over low heat approximately 5 minutes, stirring.

- Whisk in milk and cream and heat, stirring constantly, until warm.

- Stir in the spices and hot pepper sauce to taste.

- Add crab meat and heat gently. *Do not boil.* Stir in lemon juice.

- Serve in bowls garnished with a little dill.

OYSTER AND CORN CHOWDER

YIELD:
Serves 6

NOTES:
This is rich, hearty, and delicious!

24 whole shucked oysters, reserving liquid
8 tablespoons unsalted butter
4 cups corn, frozen, shucked, or freshly cut off the cob
   Do not use canned corn
1 tablespoon salt
1/2 teaspoon freshly ground pepper
1 teaspoon hot pepper sauce
4 cups heavy cream
1 1/2 cups milk
1/4 cup chopped fresh dill

- Melt butter in saucepan. Add corn, salt, pepper and hot pepper sauce.

- Sauté for 10 minutes, stirring often. If using fresh corn, cook 5 minutes longer.

- Add cream and milk and simmer slowly for 30 minutes.

- Remove from heat and cool slightly.

- Blend in food processor or blender and strain through a fine sieve.

- Heat soup and add oysters with their liquid.

- Cook just until oyster edges start to curl and adjust seasoning.

- Place 4 oysters in each of 6 soup bowls, pour soup over and garnish with dill.

MILLION DOLLAR GUMBO

YIELD:

*Makes about 8 quarts,
serving 32*

NOTES:

*Make this for the
freezer when shrimp
and crabmeat are
plentiful.*

*Serve whenever you're
having a crowd.*

12	slices bacon, cooked and drained, reserving grease
10	tablespoons flour
12	cups water
5	onions, chopped
2	green bell peppers, chopped
5	(10 ounce) packages cut frozen okra
10	bay leaves
1	teaspoon celery seed
2	teaspoons soy sauce
$1/2$	teaspoon dried tarragon
4	(16 ounce) cans tomatoes
10	tablespoons Worcestershire sauce
5	tablespoons salt
1	tablespoon freshly ground pepper
2	(6 ounce) cans tomato paste
4	shakes hot pepper sauce
$1/2$	teaspoon dried thyme
$1/2$	teaspoon dried rosemary
$1/2$	teaspoon savory
5	pounds headed raw shrimp, peeled
2	pounds backfin crab meat, cleaned (see notes, page 6)
4	tablespoons chopped fresh parsley

- In a large stockpot heat bacon grease, mixing in flour and brown, stirring constantly.

- Blend in all ingredients except bacon, shrimp, crab meat and parsley.

- Cook slowly for 2 $1/2$ hours, stirring occasionally.

- Stir in shrimp and cook until they turn pink.

- Add crab meat, bacon and parsley, stirring to combine.

SULLIVAN'S ISLAND CHOWDER

YIELD:

Serves 8

NOTES:

Live clams or oysters are best as fresh as possible. Reject those that do not have tightly closed shells or that don't snap shut when tapped.

Our choice version of an old favorite.

5 slices bacon, chopped
2 tablespoons butter
1 medium onion, chopped
2 teaspoons dried thyme
18 quahogs (large hardshell clams)
4 medium potatoes, peeled and cubed
4 cups half and half
1 tablespoon chopped parsley

- Shuck quahogs, reserving liquid.

- Poach clams in own juice, then dice, reserving liquid.

- In a large heavy pot, cook bacon until brown. Add butter, onion and thyme to bacon and sauté until onion is translucent.

- Stir in clams and their juice. Remove from heat.

- Parboil potatoes until soft. Drain and ice to stop cooking process.

- Return clam mixture to heat, add potatoes and simmer for 20 minutes.

- Warm half and half slightly. Add to warm chowder and sprinkle with parsley.

FRENCH MARKET SOUP

YIELD:

*Serves 10 -12
(Makes 6 quarts)*

NOTES:

*It should be made a
day ahead, and
freezes beautifully.*

*To make a bouquet
garni: Tie a bay leaf,
sprig of parsley,
thyme leaves and
whole peppercorns
tightly in a square of
cheesecloth.*

1   pound package 13-15 bean mix
3   ham hocks (or ham bone)
     Bouquet garni of bay leaf, thyme, parsley
1   (28 ounce) can tomatoes, chopped
2   large onions, chopped
4   stalks celery, chopped
2   cloves garlic, minced
     Salt and freshly ground pepper
1   pound kielbasa, chorizo, or Italian sausage, sliced
2   boneless chicken breasts, skinned
$1/2$ cup red wine
$1/2$ cup chopped parsley

- Wash and drain beans.

- Add beans and bouquet garni to 3 quarts water along with ham hocks (or ham bone).

- Simmer, covered, with bouquet garni for 2 to 3 hours, stirring occasionally.

- Add tomatoes, onions, celery, garlic and salt and pepper.

- Simmer, covered, for 1 $1/2$ hours.

- Add sausage and chicken breasts, and simmer about 40 minutes. Remove from heat.

- Remove chicken and ham, and bouquet garni.

- Chop chicken and return to pot.

- Refrigerate overnight.

- When ready to serve, reheat and add red wine and parsley.

ITALIAN WEDDING SOUP

YIELD:

Serves 10

NOTES:

At first glance, this may seem a daunting task. It is not as involved as it looks.
Truly a "died and gone to heaven" soup!

SOUP:

1   whole chicken
3   tablespoons chopped Italian parsley
1   large onion, coarsely chopped
4   stalks celery, leaves included, coarsely chopped
    Salt and freshly ground pepper

- In a large pot, place chicken, parsley, onion, celery, salt and pepper.
- Cover with water and simmer, covered, until chicken is tender.
- Remove chicken, strain broth and return broth to pot.
- Skin and bone chicken, cut into small pieces and reserve.

CROUTONS:

8   eggs, separated
8   tablespoons flour
1   teaspoon salt
2   teaspoons baking powder

- Beat yolks until thick.
- Beat whites until stiff.
- Fold yolks into whites, then fold in flour, salt and baking powder.
- Pour into eight-inch greased square cake pan, and bake at 350° about 30 minutes until golden.
- Cut croutons into tiny squares.

MEAT BALLS:

8   slices Italian bread
1 ½   pounds ground beef, pork and veal, combined
    Salt and freshly ground pepper
1   clove garlic, minced
1   egg, beaten
1   tablespoon freshly grated Parmesan cheese

- Pour ½ cup water on bread and squeeze it dry.

- Mix bread, meat and remaining ingredients.

- Form into tiny balls (half-inch diameter). Simmer in water to cover 30 minutes. Drain.

FINISHING TOUCHES:

8   ounces grated Parmesan cheese
1   pound fresh spinach leaves, washed and torn into pieces

- Bring chicken broth to a simmer. Add chicken and meat balls.

- Bring broth back to a simmer.

- Stir in Parmesan cheese and spinach pieces.

- Add croutons to soup and serve immediately.

CHICKEN CHOWDER

YIELD:
Serves 8

NOTES:

A perfect meal in a bowl!

For an Italian touch, add chopped Roma tomatoes and basil; or try Mexican by adding chopped green chilies and cilantro.

6   boneless chicken breasts
2   cups water
1   large onion, quartered
1   large carrot, cut into chunks
2   celery stalks, leaves included, coarsely chopped

- In a heavy pot, bring all ingredients to a boil. Reduce heat, cover and simmer $1/2$ hour, or until chicken is tender. Cool.
- Remove and cut chicken into pieces.
- Strain and reserve stock.
- Purée vegetables in blender or food processor and add to stock.

4   slices bacon
1   large onion, chopped
1   green bell pepper, seeded and chopped
2   tablespoons flour
4   potatoes, cubed
$1/4$ teaspoon hot pepper sauce
2   (9 ounce) packages frozen corn, thawed
1   pint half and half, scalded
Salt and freshly ground pepper

- In a large sauce pan fry bacon until crisp. Remove and crumble.
- Sauté onion and pepper in bacon drippings until soft.
- Stir in flour. Gradually add stock, stirring constantly, until smooth.
- Add potatoes and hot sauce, cover and simmer 10 - 15 minutes until potatoes are soft.
- Add corn and chicken and heat for 5 minutes.
- Stir in scalded half and half.
- Season to taste with salt and freshly ground pepper.
- Serve in bowls and sprinkle with crumbled bacon.

SAUSAGE AND KALE SOUP

YIELD:
Serves 8

NOTES:

Grand for good friends on a chilly evening by the fire.

If you haven't yet acquired a taste for our Southern greens, spinach can be substituted.

The Cook's Canvas *Bacon Cornbread (see page 217) is a natural accompaniment.*

1 ½ quarts chicken broth
3 cups water
½ pound kale leaves, washed and chopped fine
8 medium potatoes, peeled and diced
1 ½ pounds hot smoked sausage (or chorizo or Italian sausage)
4 cups onions, chopped
1 small green bell pepper, seeded and chopped
4 cloves garlic, finely chopped
3 tablespoons parsley, chopped
1 (28 ounce) can tomato purée
Salt and freshly ground pepper to taste.

- In a large stock pot combine broth and water. Add kale and potatoes. Bring to a boil, reduce heat, cover and simmer until potatoes are tender.

- Remove sausage casing, slice and brown in skillet.

- Remove from skillet and add to soup pot, saving drippings.

- Sauté onions, pepper and garlic in skillet in oil left from frying sausages. If skillet is too dry add 2 tablespoons olive oil.

- Stir in parsley, then add sautéed vegetables and tomato purée to soup pot.

- Simmer until vegetables are tender and tomatoes have blended well. Add salt and pepper to taste.

Edith London (born 1904)
Homage to Wilhelm Worringer, 1983
Oil on linen
Purchase of St. John's Museum of Art Memorial Acquisition Fund

Edith London was born in Germany and immigrated to the
United States shortly before the outbreak of World War II. She was
a member of Duke University's Art Department from 1955-59.

Poultry

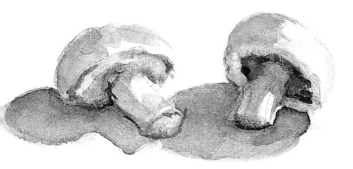

Ben Owen (1905~1984)
Jugtown Pottery, c. 1950
Bowl, platter, salt shaker and candlestick
Earthenware with clear glaze
Gift of Woodrow W. Pruett and William S. Bridges in memory of Juliana Royster Busbee

In 1921 Juliana and Jaques Busbee founded Jugtown Pottery
in Asheboro, North Carolina. In 1923, Ben Owen
joined this craft center as Jugtown's "Master Potter."

MADRAS HOT GINGER CHICKEN

YIELD:
Serves 8

NOTES:
This curry is not for the faint hearted!
It is hot, but authentic.
Mango chutney is a must.

3 tablespoons fresh ginger, grated
4 tablespoons coriander
3 tablespoons cumin
1 tablespoon cinnamon
1 1/2 teaspoons ground cloves
2 tablespoons turmeric
1 teaspoon cayenne pepper
12 black peppercorns
2 chickens, cut up and skinned
8 ounces butter
32 ounces plain yogurt
2 cups raw rice, cooked
1 cup golden raisins
2 tablespoons ground cardamom
Mango chutney as a condiment

- Grind all spices except cardamom in a blender or food processor.
- Prick chicken pieces all over with a fork.
- Rub spice mixture thoroughly into chicken and set aside for one hour.
- Melt butter in a large skillet over low heat.
- Add any remaining spice mixture, stirring, about 3 minutes.
- Add chicken, raise heat and brown.
- Stir in yogurt. Lower heat, cover and simmer for one hour.
- To warmed cooked rice add 1 cup golden raisins and stir in cardamom.
- Serve chicken over rice, spooning sauce on top.

CHICKEN OSCAR

YIELD:
Serves 4

NOTES:
A variation of the elegant classic.

12   asparagus stalks, trimmed
 4   chicken breasts, skinned, boned, and pounded flat
 2   eggs, beaten
$^1/_2$ cup flour
 4   tablespoons butter
 4   thin slices prosciutto ham
 6   ounces fresh crab meat, cleaned (see notes, page 6)
     Quick Hollandaise Sauce (see below)

- Steam asparagus and keep warm.
- Dip chicken in beaten eggs.
- Place flour on a plate, and dust chicken pieces with flour.
- Melt butter in large skillet.
- Add chicken and cook until done (4 - 5 minutes per side).
- Remove to oven-proof serving platter.
- Top each chicken breast with prosciutto.
- Arrange asparagus on top of prosciutto.
- Place crab meat over asparagus.
- Cover with Hollandaise sauce.
- Run under broiler for 45 seconds until crab meat is warm.

QUICK HOLLANDAISE SAUCE

YIELD:
Makes 1 $^1/_4$ cups

NOTES:
Another way to keep Hollandaise warm: Simply pour sauce into a wide-mouth thermos. A perfect solution if you must travel with it.

3   large egg yolks
4   teaspoons fresh lemon juice
1   cup butter, melted

- Put the egg yolks and lemon juice in a blender and cover.
- Turn blender on high.
- After 3 seconds, remove the lid and pour the butter in a steady stream over the egg mixture.
- Serve at once or keep warm by immersing blender container in warm water.

LEMON LOVERS' CHICKEN

YIELD:
Serves 6

NOTES:
We think this is one of the best chicken recipes we have ever tried!

6 chicken breasts, skinned and boned
2 cups fresh lemon juice (9 to 10 lemons)
1 cup flour
1 1/2 teaspoons salt
2 teaspoons paprika
1 teaspoon freshly ground pepper
1/2 cup olive oil
2 tablespoons grated lemon zest
1/3 cup packed light brown sugar
1/4 cup chicken broth
2 lemons, sliced
Parsley, minced

- In large zip-lock bag, place chicken and lemon juice. Squeeze out all possible air. Refrigerate overnight, turning once.

- Remove chicken, pat dry. Reserve 2 tablespoons marinade.

- Put flour, salt, paprika and pepper in a plastic bag. Shake until well mixed.

- Place chicken in bag, one piece at a time, and shake to coat evenly.

- Heat oil in large skillet and fry chicken until well browned.

- Arrange chicken in one layer in a large baking dish.

- Sprinkle evenly with lemon zest and brown sugar.

- Mix chicken broth with reserved marinade and pour around chicken.

- Place a lemon slice on each chicken breast and sprinkle with parsley.

- Bake at 350° for 20 - 30 minutes.

PORT CITY CHICKEN

YIELD:
Serves 4

NOTES:
Delicate flavors surround this moist chicken.

Celery root, also known as celeriac, gives this its unique taste.

4	skinless boneless chicken breasts
	Salt and freshly ground pepper
2	tablespoons flour
2	tablespoons oil, divided
2	tablespoons butter, divided
3	cups celery root, peeled and julienned
1	medium onion, chopped
1	medium red bell pepper, chopped
2	tablespoons chopped fresh parsley
1	tablespoon lemon juice
$1/3$	cup heavy cream
$1/2$	teaspoon hot pepper sauce
$1/4$	teaspoon dry mustard
2	tablespoons Dijon mustard
$1/4$	teaspoon freshly ground pepper
$1/2$	cup shredded Monterey Jack (or white cheddar) cheese

- Pat chicken dry and sprinkle with salt and pepper. Dust with flour.

- Heat 1 tablespoon oil and 1 tablespoon butter in large skillet over medium heat.

- Brown chicken on both sides, lower heat and sauté 5 - 10 minutes, or until cooked. Remove from pan and keep warm.

- Add remaining oil and butter to skillet. Sauté celery root, onion and red pepper about 2 minutes. Cover and simmer until vegetables are tender, approximately 15 minutes.

- Stir in parsley, lemon juice, cream, hot pepper sauce, dry mustard, Dijon mustard and pepper.

- Return chicken to pan and heat about 2 minutes.

- Spread vegetables in oven-proof serving dish and top with chicken.

- Sprinkle with cheese and run under broiler for a minute to melt cheese.

APPLE CIDER CHICKEN

YIELD:

Serves 4

NOTES:

A wonderful cold weather dish.

It smells like fall and football games!

A 3-pound chicken, quartered and skinned
1 cup apple cider
1/2 cup flour
1 teaspoon cinnamon
1 teaspoon ground ginger
Salt and freshly ground pepper
2 tablespoons brown sugar
1 apple, cored and sliced
2 tablespoons honey

- Marinate chicken in cider for 1 hour.

- Remove chicken and reserve cider.

- In a small bowl, mix flour, cinnamon, ginger, salt and pepper.

- Dredge the chicken in the flour mixture.

- Place chicken in a shallow baking dish.

- Bake chicken 40 minutes at 350°.

- Combine reserved cider, brown sugar, apple slices and honey in a small bowl.

- Pour this mixture over chicken.

- Bake for an additional 20 minutes at 350°. Serve immediately with rice or noodles.

CHICKEN MARSALA

YIELD:

Serves 6

NOTES:

*Our presentation
of fanning the chicken
slices is more appealing
than placing the whole
chicken breast on a
plate.*

*For any sauced
chicken dish, sprinkle
the top with paprika
before serving.*

6   slices prosciutto

6   boneless, skinless chicken breasts, flattened to
even thickness

2   ounces Fontina cheese, cubed

6   tablespoons Parmesan cheese

6   large fresh sage leaves

1   tablespoon olive oil

1   tablespoon butter

1   cup Marsala wine

1   cup chicken stock

1   cup cream

- Place one piece of prosciutto on top of each chicken breast.

- Top each with Fontina and Parmesan, then put one sage leaf over cheeses.

- Tuck in sides of breasts, roll into a bundle and tie, or secure with toothpicks.

- Brown in oil and butter (you might need to add more butter in the browning process).

- Pour Marsala and stock over chicken. Cover and simmer 15 - 20 minutes.

- Remove chicken and reduce sauce until thickened.

- Carefully stir in 1 cup cream.

- Remove ties or toothpicks, and slice breasts in $1/2$-inch pieces and serve fanned on a plate with polenta or rice and sauce.

APRICOT CHICKEN

YIELD:
Serves 8

NOTES:
Wonderful to have when you're running late.

Can be very elegant served with couscous.

1 tablespoon olive oil
$^1/_2$ cup flour
1 teaspoon salt
Freshly ground pepper to taste
8 chicken breasts, skinned
$^1/_2$ cup apricot preserves
1 tablespoon Dijon mustard
$^1/_2$ cup non-fat plain yogurt
2 tablespoons sliced almonds

- Grease a shallow baking pan with oil.
- Put flour, salt and pepper in a plastic bag, add chicken pieces and shake until chicken is coated.
- Shake off excess flour and bake chicken in oiled pan for 25 minutes at 375°.
- Mix preserves, mustard and yogurt and spread on chicken.
- Sprinkle with almonds and bake an additional 30 minutes.

PAPRIKASH BUDAPEST

YIELD:
Serves 8

NOTES:
Green peppercorns grow in the Spice Islands. Do not substitute dried peppercorns.

Best served with green spinach noodles.

2	whole chickens, skinned and cut up
³/₄	cup flour
2	tablespoons Hungarian paprika
2	tablespoons olive oil
8	scallions, including green tops, chopped
5	oil-packed sun-dried tomatoes, chopped
2	teaspoons (packed in brine) green peppercorns
1	cup tomato ketchup diluted with 1 ¹/₂ cups water
1	cup sour cream
	Salt and freshly ground pepper to taste

- Shake chicken pieces in a plastic bag with combined flour and paprika.

- Heat oil in a heavy pot and brown chicken until it is reddish gold and starting to crust.

- Add scallions, sun-dried tomatoes and peppercorns.

- Stir in diluted ketchup, lower heat and simmer 45 minutes.

- Add sour cream and heat through, stirring.

CHICKEN A L'ORANGE

YIELD:

Serves 4

NOTES:

This well seasoned chicken can easily be cooked on the grill. Just brush the chicken with the chutney mixture in the last part of cooking time to keep chutney from burning.

A 3-pound chicken, skinned and quartered
Juice of one large orange
$^1/_2$ cup white wine
$^3/_4$ cup fruit chutney
  2   teaspoons freshly ground mixed peppercorns
$^1/_4$ cup Dijon mustard

- Marinate chicken in orange juice and wine at least one hour.

- Combine chutney, pepper and mustard in small saucepan and heat.

- Arrange chicken in casserole, reserving marinade.

- Coat with chutney mixture and pour marinade over chicken.

- Bake uncovered, for 45 minutes at 350°, turning once.

MARMALADE GINGER CHICKEN

YIELD:

Serves 4

NOTES:

This is a flavorful, easy entrée.

To have fresh ginger always on hand: Peel, cut in pieces, and store in a jar full of dry sherry. Tightly cover jar and keep refrigerated.

Use sherry in salad dressings.

4   chicken breasts, boneless and skinless
4   tablespoons orange marmalade
4   tablespoons orange juice
1   teaspoon ground ginger (or 1 tablespoon minced fresh ginger)
2   teaspoons Worcestershire sauce
1   teaspoon Dijon mustard
1   clove garlic, minced

- Put chicken in a shallow baking dish which has been prepared with a non-stick spray.

- Combine remaining ingredients in a small bowl.

- Spread evenly over chicken.

- Bake at 350° for 45 minutes, uncovered, basting occasionally.

FRIED CHICKEN

YIELD:

Serves 6

NOTES:

We can't have a Southern cookbook without Fried Chicken.

The hot sauce makes it crispy, not fiery. Try it!

When you are frying, and oil spatters, put a small crouton in the pan.

12   chicken pieces, skin on
      Seasoned salt of choice
1   (5 ounce) bottle mild red hot sauce
      Flour for dredging
      Solid white shortening

- Rinse chicken pieces and pat dry.

- Sprinkle with seasoned salt.

- Put in a bowl and marinate in hot sauce for 30 minutes.

- Put chicken pieces and flour in a paper or plastic bag and shake to coat.

- In a heavy skillet, heat enough shortening to cover one-half side of chicken pieces.

- Fry chicken until golden brown on one side, then turn over and continue until both sides are evenly browned and chicken is cooked through.

- Drain on paper towels.

CHICKEN BREASTS ÉTOUFFÉES

YIELD:

Serves 6

NOTES:

Our testers were divided as to which stuffing was best. You decide. Shrimp or mushrooms? In either case, this is an elegant dish.

6 chicken boneless breasts, skinned and pounded to an even thickness
4 cups cooked shrimp (or sliced raw mushrooms)
2 cups chopped scallions with green tops

• Mix shrimp (or mushrooms) with scallions.

MORNAY SAUCE :

$^1/_2$ cup butter
$^1/_2$ cup flour
2 $^1/_2$ cups light cream (or milk)
1 teaspoon fresh basil
$^1/_2$ teaspoon salt
1 teaspoon dried dill
$^1/_2$ cup dry white wine
2 cups grated Swiss cheese

• Melt butter in saucepan.

• Mix flour with butter over low heat.

• Slowly add cream (or milk), basil, salt and dill, stirring constantly, until sauce is smooth.

• Continue cooking until sauce is thick. Add wine and cheese.

• Cook, stirring, until cheese is melted.

TO ASSEMBLE:

• Stir half the Mornay sauce into shrimp (or mushroom) mixture.

• Place equal portions of shrimp (or mushrooms) on chicken breasts.

• Roll chicken around stuffing and place seam side down in greased casserole.

• Pour remaining sauce over chicken and bake at 375° for 20 to 25 minutes.

LEMON ROASTED CHICKEN

YIELD:

Serves 4

NOTES:

*This is also very
successful with
Cornish game hens.*

A 5-pound roasting chicken

2 large lemons, thinly sliced and seeded

3 tablespoons fresh rosemary leaves (or 2 teaspoons dried)

1 ½ teaspoons salt

¼ teaspoon freshly ground black pepper

- Gently loosen the skin from the meat with your fingers, starting at the body cavity and working toward the neck.

- Rub the chicken meat under the skin with rosemary.

- Slip as many lemon slices under the skin as it takes to cover the meat.

- Pat the skin in place and put any remaining slices in the cavity.

- Sprinkle the skin with salt and pepper. Put chicken in a roasting pan breast side up and bake at 450°.

- Immediately turn the heat down to 350° and roast 20 minutes per pound, basting occasionally, or until tender. Serve with pan juices.

CARIBBEAN CHICKEN

YIELD:

Serves 4 - 6

NOTES:

The flavors are somewhat exotic and definitely call for the dark meat of the chicken.

8   pieces of dark meat chicken, skinned
     Salt and freshly ground pepper, to taste
1   tablespoon olive oil
1   large onion, chopped
2   cloves garlic, chopped
2   tablespoons finely chopped fresh ginger
1   cup dark rum
2   cups chicken stock
$1/2$ cup heavy cream
1   large tomato, peeled and quartered
1   ripe mango, cut into slices (if fresh is not available, use jarred, draining syrup)
1   ripe banana, cut into $1/2$ inch slices

- Sprinkle chicken with salt and pepper.

- Heat oil in heavy-bottomed casserole. Brown chicken over medium heat, about five minutes.

- Add onion and cook with chicken until onion is translucent. Add garlic and ginger and cook one minute more.

- Remove casserole from heat until slightly cooled.

- Add rum and return to heat and simmer until liquid is reduced.

- Add stock and simmer until chicken juices run clear.

- Transfer chicken to warm serving platter and cover with foil.

- In a saucepan, bring cream and tomato to a simmer.

- Pour in the liquid from casserole and simmer until it thickens slightly.

- Purée liquid in food processor and return to pan.

- Add mango and banana and cook one minute.

- Remove the foil from the chicken and pour the sauce over the pieces.

HONEYED CHICKEN BREASTS

YIELD:

Serves 4 - 6

NOTES:

This is tender and moist.

It's elegant enough for company, but easy enough for the family. Serve with wild rice.

6 chicken breasts, skinned, split and boned
Salt and freshly ground pepper
$^1/_2$ cup vegetable oil
1 cup coarse bread crumbs
$^1/_2$ teaspoon thyme
$^1/_2$ teaspoon oregano
$^3/_4$ cup honey
$^1/_4$ cup prepared Dijon mustard
$^1/_4$ cup prepared horseradish
$^1/_2$ cup white wine

- Season chicken with salt and pepper.
- Brush chicken with oil.
- Coat each piece with bread crumbs.
- Place chicken in baking dish in one layer.
- Combine spices, honey, mustard and horseradish.
- Pour wine and honey mixture over chicken.
- Bake at 375° for 40 minutes, or until golden.

STIR-FRY CHICKEN WITH PEPPER SAUCE

YIELD:

Serves 4

NOTES:

Stir fry cooking is gloriously quick.

Red pepper strips, snow peas, and/or small broccoli flowerets can be added at the same time as chicken for crunch and color.

Try this with shrimp instead of chicken.

4 boneless chicken breasts
1 tablespoon finely chopped fresh ginger
1 clove garlic, crushed
4 scallions, chopped in $1/4$ inch lengths
$1/4$ teaspoon crushed red pepper flakes
1 teaspoon corn starch
3 tablespoons chicken stock (or water)
3 tablespoons dry sherry
2 tablespoons soy sauce
1 teaspoon sugar
$1/2$ teaspoon salt
2 tablespoons oil

- Cut chicken into $1/2$ inch cubes and refrigerate.

- In a small bowl combine ginger, garlic, scallions and red pepper.

- In a second bowl, combine corn starch with stock (or water), then add sherry, soy sauce, sugar and salt.

- Heat wok or skillet to medium high. Add oil.

- Pour in ginger mixture. Stir fry 20 seconds and add chicken pieces. Stir fry 2 minutes.

- Stir corn starch mixture and pour into wok stirring continuously until mixture thickens and coats chicken with translucent glaze. *Do not overcook.*

- Serve at once over rice.

BAYOU BEND CHICKEN

YIELD:
Serves 6

NOTES:
Most unusual and wonderful.

3 pounds selected chicken pieces, skinned and boned
4 tablespoons butter
1 cup beef broth
1 teaspoon dried bouquet garni
$^2/_3$ cup whipping cream
1 pint oysters

- Drain oysters, do not rinse, but check for shells.
- Brown chicken in butter, adding more butter if necessary.
- Place in oven-proof casserole.
- Pour broth over chicken and sprinkle with herbs.
- Bake, covered, at 375° for 40 minutes.
- In a saucepan, warm the cream and add the oysters.
- Pour cream and oysters over chicken and bake at 350° for an additional 10 minutes, or just long enough to curl the edges of the oysters.
- Serve immediately.

FRIDAY AFTER THANKSGIVING TURKEY

YIELD:
Serves 6

NOTES:

A change from turkey hash for left-overs.

For brunch, pan-fry turkey patties, top each with poached egg, and our Quick Hollandaise (see page 48).

2 cups diced, cooked, cold turkey
1 cup left-over turkey dressing
2 eggs, well-beaten
$^1/_2$ cup turkey gravy
  Béchamel Sauce (see below)
  Harvest Cranberry Sauce (see page 66) for garnish

- Combine all ingredients except Béchamel and cranberry sauce.

- Mold into 6 well-rounded patties and place in a greased baking dish.

- Pour béchamel sauce around patties and bake at 350° until brown.

- Just before serving, place a dab of cranberry sauce on top of each patty.

BÉCHAMEL SAUCE

YIELD:
Makes 1 cup

NOTES:

To make a unique macaroni and cheese add your favorite cheese, crisp bacon and chopped tomato to this sauce. Pour over cooked pasta and bake until bubbly.

2 tablespoons butter
2 tablespoons flour
$^1/_2$ cup half and half, heated
$^1/_2$ cup chicken (or turkey) stock
  Salt
  Paprika
1 egg, beaten

- Melt butter and stir in flour.

- Slowly add half and half and stock, stirring constantly until thick.

- Add salt to taste and paprika.

- Beat a little of the hot mixture into the egg, then combine with remaining sauce.

- Stir over very low heat. Do not allow to boil.

SANTA YNEZ TURKEY

YIELD:
Serves 4

NOTES:
The tang of the turkey marries well with the fruity salsa.

4   skinless turkey breast fillets, each about 3/4 inch thick.
4   ounces mild green hot sauce
    Pineapple Salsa (see below)

- Place turkey fillets in glass dish and coat with mild green hot sauce.
- Cover and refrigerate for 2 hours.
- Grill or broil until juices run clear, about 7 minutes per side.
- Transfer to serving plates and serve immediately with the pineapple salsa.

PINEAPPLE SALSA

YIELD:
Makes about 1 1/2 cups

NOTES:
Ham lovers! Try this salsa as a condiment.

1   small pineapple, peeled, cored, and chopped
1/2 cup minced red onion
1/2 cup minced fresh cilantro
2   tablespoons minced fresh mint
1   tablespoon white wine vinegar
    Salt and freshly ground pepper

- In a glass serving bowl, mix all ingredients.
- Cover and refrigerate 2 - 4 hours.

TURKEY PICADILLO

YIELD:
Serves 20

NOTES:

An exciting, healthy alternative to spaghetti with meat sauce.

Easy to make ahead and serve after a game.

Makes great "Sloppy Joes".

8 pounds ground turkey
2 cups dry sherry
$^1/_2$ cup olive oil
3 cups minced onion
3 cups minced green pepper
1 tablespoon minced garlic
2 cups chopped pimiento stuffed olives
1 cup tomato paste
6 tablespoons capers
2 tablespoons chili powder
2 teaspoons ground cumin
Salt and freshly ground pepper to taste
1 cup slivered blanched almonds, toasted

- Marinate the turkey in the sherry for 30 minutes.

- Heat the oil in a very large heavy pot.

- Sauté onions and peppers until onions are lightly browned, stirring constantly.

- Stir in the garlic.

- Add the turkey and sauté, stirring until the excess liquid has evaporated - approximately 10 minutes.

- Add remaining ingredients, except almonds and cook about 15 minutes.

- Serve over rice, pasta or noodles. Sprinkle with the almonds.

HARVEST CRANBERRY SAUCE

YIELD:
Makes 6 cups

NOTES:
The nuts add a crunch to this variation of a holiday classic.

4 cups fresh cranberries, rinsed and stems removed
2 cups water
1 ½ cups sugar
1 cup raisins
1 cup coarsely chopped walnuts

- Boil cranberries in water until the cranberry skins pop.
- Add sugar and raisins and boil an additional 10 minutes.
- Stir in nuts.
- Pour into jars and refrigerate, or pour into sterilized jars and seal.

PEAR CHUTNEY

YIELD:
2 quarts

NOTES:
Make chutney when pears are plentiful and serve at holidays in place of cranberry sauce.

4 cups pears, peeled and diced
1 cup roasted, peeled and diced red peppers
1 cup diced onions
1 cup chopped pecans
¾ cup cider vinegar
½ cup honey
½ cup brown sugar
⅓ cup preserved ginger, cut
1 tablespoon salt
1 tablespoon or less of hot pepper sauce
5 cloves
1 cinnamon stick
¾ cup currants

- In a large pot, cook peppers and onions in vinegar on low heat until soft.
- Add other ingredients and simmer one hour.
- Pack while hot in sterilized jars and seal; or cool, pour into jars and refrigerate.

LOUISIANA GAME HENS

YIELD:

Serves 6

NOTES:

This is also a delectable way to prepare quail.

Either way, served with Nutty Wild Rice (see page 146) and broiled tomatoes, it makes an elegant presentation.

1   pound lean bulk sausage
6   Cornish game hens, rinsed and patted dry
6   slices bacon
$^1/_4$ cup butter, divided
$^1/_4$ cup all-purpose flour
2   cups red wine
2   tablespoons red currant jelly
$^1/_2$ teaspoon salt
$^1/_4$ teaspoon pepper

- Spoon sausage into body cavity of hens.

- Wrap each hen with a piece of bacon and secure with a toothpick.

- Melt 1 tablespoon butter in large skillet, add hens one at a time, and brown on all sides.

- Place in a baking dish large enough to contain the hens.

- Combine remaining 3 tablespoons butter with pan drippings in skillet, add flour and stir until smooth.

- Cook one minute over medium heat and gradually add wine, stirring constantly until thickened and bubbling.

- Stir in jelly, salt and pepper.

- When jelly has melted, pour over hens and bake at 325° for 45 to 60 minutes.

ROASTED WILD DUCK

2	ducks, cleaned and blotted dry
$^1/_2$	teaspoon salt
1	teaspoon fresh minced ginger
1	teaspoon basil
$^1/_4$	teaspoon pepper
$^1/_8$	teaspoon dry mustard
1	clove garlic, minced
1	teaspoon brown sugar
6	tablespoons soy sauce
2	tablespoons olive oil
2	tablespoons white wine (or vermouth)
2	teaspoons balsamic vinegar
3	tablespoons orange juice
1 - 2	oranges, sliced $^1/_2$ inch thick

- Mix dry herbs, spices, garlic and ginger together. Sprinkle $^1/_2$ inside cavity of birds.

- Combine liquids with brown sugar and spoon $^1/_3$ of mixture into cavities along with orange slices.

- Rub remaining dry seasoning mixture on outside of ducks.

- Place each bird, breast side down, on a large piece of heavy duty aluminum foil and pour rest of liquid over ducks.

- Tightly seal ducks in the foil.

- Place in a roasting pan and roast at 325° for two hours.

- Unwrap and baste with drippings, reseal foil and bake another 15 to 20 minutes.

HUNTER'S MARINADE

YIELD:

Makes about 3 cups

NOTES:

This marinade and sauce are also excellent with pork or chicken.

2 cups rice vinegar
   Juice of two lemons
2 tablespoons red pepper flakes
2 tablespoons soy sauce
$1/2$ cup Worcestershire sauce
1 tablespoon salt
$1/2$ cup chopped parsley
2 cloves garlic, crushed
$1/2$ cup currant jelly
$1/2$ cup brandy

- Combine all but last 2 ingredients in a saucepan and bring to a boil.
- Use as marinade for game birds.
- For a sauce add jelly and brandy to marinade.
- Boil to reduce slightly.

BASTING SAUCE FOR CHICKEN

YIELD:

1 $1/2$ cups sauce

NOTES:

For a summertime barbeque select your favorite pieces of chicken and heat up the grill.

1 cup clover honey
1 tablespoon rum
2 tablespoons Dijon mustard
$1/4$ cup teriyaki sauce
1 tablespoon dark molasses
2 tablespoons ketchup

- Combine all ingredients.
- Marinate chicken in sauce for at least 4 hours.
- Place on preheated grill, basting every 5 minutes. Turn after 10 minutes.
- Grill until juices run clear when pierced by a fork.

Elliott Daingerfield (1859~1932)
Approaching Storm, 1905
Oil on board
Gift of St. John's Museum of Art Volunteer Guild

Born in Fayettville, NC, Elliott Daingerfield
became the South's most noted painter of his era.

Meats

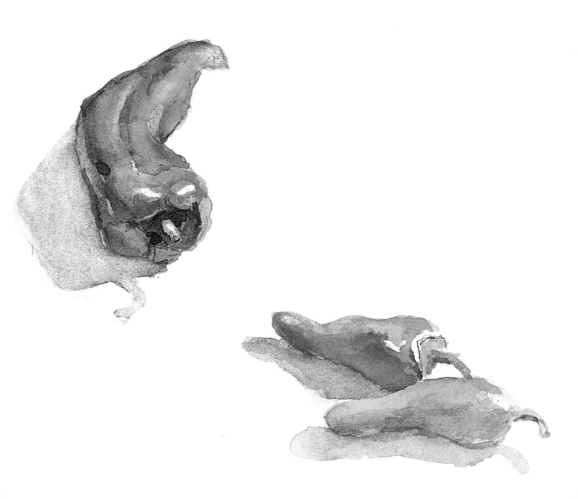

Jacob Marling (1744~1833)
Portrait of a Gentleman, c. 1800
Oil on canvas
Gift of Mr. and Mrs. James E. Hall

Jacob Marling was an itinerant artist who recorded
the images of many noted Carolinians.

ROLLED PORK LOIN IN APRICOT SAUCE

YIELD:

Serves 6

NOTES:

A very elegant presentation.

2   cups dry white wine
4   tablespoons orange liqueur
2   cups dried apricots
1   3 ½ pound center cut pork loin, which has been split in two pieces
1   red onion, thinly sliced
1   teaspoon fresh lemon thyme
1   teaspoon fresh marjoram
1   teaspoon fresh oregano
1   tablespoon fresh basil
4   tablespoons butter
4   tablespoons oil
2   cups beef broth
4   tablespoons corn starch

- Combine wine, liqueur and apricots. Soak 4 hours or overnight.
- Remove apricots, reserving liquid for sauce.
- Butterfly each pork piece, slashing across grain to make even in thickness.
- Place onion slices evenly over each piece of meat.
- Sprinkle onions with herbs and top with apricots overlapping, down the center.
- Close butterflied pieces and tie tightly with string at intervals, making sure apricots are secured.
- Heat butter and oil in heavy oven-proof pan.
- On top of stove brown meat on all sides then roast in 375° oven until meat thermometer reaches 150°.
- Remove meat from pan, reserving juices.
- Add apricot liquid to pan, along with beef broth and corn starch.
- Heat and whisk until liquid is smooth and thick.
- Remove string. Slice meat and serve with sauce.

OAXACAN PORK

YIELD:
Serves 8

NOTES:
This dish has a beautiful presentation with carrots and peppers in the center of each pork slice.
Sauce is delicious.

A 4-pound pork loin, butterflied
3   carrots, julienned
2   red bell peppers, julienned
1 1/2 tablespoons freshly ground coriander seeds
1 1/2 tablespoons freshly ground cumin
     Salt and freshly ground pepper to taste
5   tablespoons olive oil
1   large onion, chopped
2   cloves garlic, minced
3   cups milk, heated
1/4   cup cold milk, optional
1   teaspoon corn starch, optional
     Chopped cilantro (or parsley) for garnish

- Place carrots and peppers on top of meat.

- Place ground spices and salt and pepper over carrots and peppers.

- Let stand at least 30 minutes at room temperature.

- Roll pork with vegetables inside and tie with string in several places.

- In a skillet large enough to hold pork, brown onion and garlic in oil. Brown pork on all sides.

- Add heated milk and simmer, uncovered, until web forms.

- Turn heat very low and cook until meat thermometer reads 150°. It should cook in about 2 - 2 1/2 hours. Remove pork, let stand 20 minutes, cut off strings, and slice.

- Sauce will appear curdled. If this is offensive, stir in corn starch mixed with cold milk and whisk into sauce.

- Serve pork slices on a bed of rice or polenta, and pour sauce over top. Sprinkle with cilantro (or parsley) for garnish.

MAHOGANY PORK CHOPS

YIELD:

Serves 6

NOTES:

Interesting, exotic flavors.

12 pork chops, thinly sliced
3/4 teaspoon salt
Freshly ground black pepper
1 tablespoon cracked coriander seeds
1 tablespoon ground cumin seeds
1/2 cup salad oil (or more)
1 tablespoon brown sugar
1/2 cup sliced shallots (or onion)
4 tablespoons soy sauce
1 tablespoon freshly grated ginger
Juice of 2 limes

- Put chops and next five ingredients in large bowl. Stir to coat meat and let stand 20 minutes. If meat is not shiny, add a little more oil.

- Add remaining ingredients and stir well. Let stand at least one hour.

- Broil or grill chops 2 - 3 minutes per side.

PORK LOIN IN RED WINE SAUCE

YIELD:
Serves 6

NOTES:
This is rich and wonderful.

PORK:

2	(1 pound) pork tenderloins
	Freshly ground pepper
2	tablespoons butter
2	tablespoons oil
1/2	cup red wine
1/2	cup chicken stock
4	tablespoons chopped fresh basil

- Rub pork tenderloins with freshly ground pepper.
- In a large saucepan, melt butter, add oil and brown pork quickly.
- Remove saucepan from heat and carefully add red wine, stock and basil.
- Cover and cook over low heat 30 - 45 minutes, or until meat thermometer reads 150°.
- Remove meat from pan, keeping warm.
- Reserve 1/3 cup pan drippings.
- Slice pork thinly and serve with sauce on the side.

SAUCE:

1	cup red wine
2	tablespoon corn starch
6	tablespoons water
1/3	cup reserved pan drippings

- In a small saucepan, combine first three ingredients.
- Mix with a wire whisk until corn starch is dissolved.
- Stir in reserved drippings and cook until thickened.

CRANBERRY PORK

YIELD:

Serves 6

NOTES:

If you buy an extra bag of cranberries for the freezer when they're in season, this is an all-year dish.

6 lean, thick, boneless pork chops, at room temperature
1 ½ tablespoons olive oil
1 large onion, coarsely chopped
²/₃ cup ketchup
½ cup brown sugar, firmly packed
2 tablespoons balsamic vinegar
2 teaspoons Dijon mustard
2 cups fresh cranberries

- Preheat oven to 400°.
- In a large hot skillet, sear chops quickly on both sides.
- In a 9" x 13" greased baking pan, arrange pork in one layer.
- Bake uncovered for 15 minutes.
- Add oil to skillet and sauté onion until golden, stirring occasionally.
- Add remaining ingredients, blending thoroughly.
- Spoon onion-cranberry mixture evenly over pork.
- Continue baking about 20 - 25 minutes longer, or until cranberries have begun to caramelize.

PORK CHOPS WITH SAVORY SAUCE

YIELD:

Serves 4

NOTES:

Try cooking pork chops while sauce is being reduced to make it even quicker!

$^3/_4$ cup chicken stock
$^1/_4$ cup raspberry (or Balsamic) vinegar
4 teaspoons olive oil
2 tablespoons red wine
1 teaspoon sugar
$^1/_2$ teaspoon oregano
1 garlic clove, minced
1 teaspoon corn starch
2 tablespoons cold water
2 teaspoons oil
4 boneless pork chops, all fat removed

- Combine first seven ingredients in small saucepan.
- Cook until liquid is reduced to $^1/_2$ cup.
- Mix corn starch with water and add to pan.
- Stir until mixture thickens (about one minute) and set aside.
- Pan-fry pork chops in oil.
- When pork is cooked to your taste, serve with sauce.

TANGY COUSCOUS WITH PORK

YIELD:

Serves 4

NOTES:

This is a light and delicious meal.

Can use left-over pork roast, thinly sliced.

PORK:

1 ½   pounds pork tenderloin, cut in ¼-inch slices
        Juice of one lemon
1   tablespoon cumin
2   tablespoons oil

- Rub lemon juice and cumin into pork slices.
- Brown meat on both sides in 2 tablespoons oil.
- Set aside to cool.

COUSCOUS:

1   tablespoon olive oil
1   pound mushrooms, sliced
1   cup chopped onion
1   garlic clove, minced
2   cups chicken broth
½   cup golden raisins
½   cup chopped parsley
½   cup chopped mint
2   tablespoons grated lemon zest
1   large tomato, peeled and chopped
1   cup couscous
½   teaspoon cayenne pepper, or to taste
        Salt and freshly ground pepper to taste

- Heat oil in large pot. Sauté mushrooms, onions and garlic until soft.
- Add chicken broth, raisins, parsley, mint, lemon zest and tomato.
- Bring to a boil.
- Stir in couscous, cover, and turn off heat.
- Let stand 3 to 5 minutes. Spoon onto serving platter.
- Place cooked pork on top of couscous.
- Add salt and pepper to taste.

VINDALOO LAMB CURRY

YIELD:

Serves 8

NOTES:

Raisins, sliced ginger, crumbled crisp bacon, toasted coconut, chopped peanuts, diced tomatoes are some condiment options.

If you like your curry hot, add red pepper to taste, but be careful!

Serve with saffron rice or roasted potatoes and a good chutney.

3	pounds boneless lamb, cut in 2" cubes
1/3	cup white wine vinegar
2	teaspoons salt
1/2	teaspoon black pepper
5	tablespoons curry powder (hot Madras, if available)
1 1/2	teaspoons cinnamon
1	cup flour
4	tablespoons butter
4	tablespoons oil
2	medium onions, finely chopped
3	tablespoons chopped garlic
2	tablespoons chopped fresh ginger
1/2 to 1	teaspoon cayenne pepper (optional)
1 1/2	cups chicken broth
8	ounces unsweetened coconut milk
	Mango chutney

- Marinate lamb in white wine vinegar, salt and pepper for about 3 hours at room temperature. Drain and pat dry with paper towels.

- Mix curry powder, cinnamon and flour together in small bowl.

- Dip lamb in flour mixture and coat each piece.

- Brown quickly in oil and butter in large deep skillet, and remove from pan.

- Add onions, garlic, ginger, cayenne pepper and cook over low heat, stirring.

- Add broth and coconut milk. Stir until thickened.

- Add lamb and any juices that may have accumulated, cover and simmer 30 minutes, adding water if necessary.

- Serve with chutney and other condiments.

ROASTED COFFEE LAMB

YIELD:

Serves 8

NOTES:

These unusual flavors are Swedish in origin.

Ask your butcher to butterfly the lamb.

A 6-pound leg of lamb, boned and butterflied
1 tablespoon salt
2 tablespoons Dijon mustard
2 large onions, sliced
4 carrots, sliced
1/2 cup chopped fresh rosemary, parsley, and thyme, combined
3 cloves garlic, minced
1 cup beef stock
1 cup very strong black coffee (made from instant coffee, twice as strong as usual)
1/2 cup heavy cream
1/2 cup brandy
2 tablespoons red currant jelly

- Open out lamb and spread inside with salt and mustard.
- Place onions and carrots evenly on top, sprinkle with herbs and garlic. Roll up like a jelly roll, tying with string in several places.
- Mix stock, coffee, cream and brandy.
- Roast in 425° oven for 30 minutes.
- Reduce oven temperature to 350°.
- Pour coffee mixture over lamb and bake 50 minutes longer, basting frequently.
- Remove lamb to warm serving platter and tent with foil.
- Before serving, remove strings and slice.
- Strain sauce, return to pan, add currant jelly and stir over low heat until jelly is melted. Serve separately from meat.

PERSIAN LAMB

YIELD:

Serves 6

NOTES:

A delectable blend of Middle Eastern flavors.

A pretty dinner party treat, possibly served with minted peas.

2 pounds boneless lamb, cut from leg into 1-inch cubes
  Flour for dredging
3 tablespoons olive oil
1/2 cup chopped onion
1 tablespoon minced fresh ginger
1 teaspoon ground cinnamon
1/2 teaspoon cumin
1 (10 1/2 ounce) can chicken broth
2 fresh peaches, cut in wedges (or 6 dried apricots, cut up)
1/4 cup slivered almonds
1 tablespoon butter
1/2 cup golden raisins

- Coat lamb pieces with flour.

- In large skillet, brown lamb in oil. Remove from skillet.

- Sauté onion in same oil until golden.

- Add ginger, cinnamon, cumin, lamb and chicken broth.

- Cover and simmer 15 - 20 minutes until lamb is tender, stirring and adding water if too dry.

- Add peaches (or apricots) and simmer 3 or 4 minutes.

- Sauté almonds in butter until browned, add raisins and sprinkle over lamb.

- Serve with rice or couscous mounded around the lamb and sauce on the side.

SAUCE:

1 cup plain yogurt
1/4 teaspoon cinnamon
4 tablespoons lemon juice

- Combine all sauce ingredients.

GINGERED LAMB SHANKS

YIELD:

Serves 6

NOTES:

Lamb shanks are one of our favorites!

Braising for several hours allows the lamb shanks to become meaty and tender.

6 lamb shanks
Salt and freshly ground pepper
Flour for dredging
2 medium onions, chopped
2 cloves garlic, minced
1 cup white wine
1/4 cup soy sauce
Juice of 2 lemons
1/4 cup minced ginger
4 tablespoons dark brown sugar

- Season lamb shanks with salt and pepper.

- Roll lamb shanks in flour, shaking off excess.

- Place shanks in a single layer, in a 9" x 13" pan. Cover with chopped onions and garlic .

- Bake uncovered at 400° for about 20 minutes.

- Turn shanks over and add wine, soy sauce, lemon juice, ginger and brown sugar.

- Cover pan tightly with foil, reduce heat to 300° and bake for an additional 1 1/2 to 2 hours, checking liquid level occasionally. Shanks should be very tender.

- If liquid is evaporating too quickly, add water or more wine.

- Arrange shanks in a spoke pattern over a bed of rice or noodles.

INDONESIAN FIRE MOUTH (Satay Kambing Hadura)

YIELD:
Serves 6

NOTES:

Lamb may be broiled on bamboo skewers, which have been soaked in water for 30 minutes.

Served with beer, this is flavorful as an entrée or an appetizer.

When cooking very spicy food, like chili or curries, always add a sweetener to the sauce. It brings out the flavor.

$^1/_2$ cup soy sauce
1 teaspoon ground red pepper
$^1/_3$ cup smooth peanut butter
1 clove garlic, minced
    Juice of one lemon
1 teaspoon molasses
$^3/_4$ cup hot water
$^1/_2$ cup ground roasted peanuts
3 pounds lamb, cubed

- In a saucepan combine all ingredients except lamb.
- Bring to a boil, stirring until smooth, and allow to cool.
- Pour half the peanut sauce over lamb and stir to coat meat. Let stand one hour. Remove meat and reserve marinade.
- Broil lamb, and serve with the following sauce.

SAUCE:

Reserved peanut sauce and marinade
$^1/_2$ cup tomato sauce
    Juice of one lemon
    Dash of hot red pepper sauce
$^1/_4$ cup water

- To the remaining peanut sauce and marinade, add all sauce ingredients.
- Bring to a boil, stirring, and serve on the side.

QUICK SAUERBRATEN

YIELD:

Serves 6

NOTES:

*Serve over wide egg
noodles, garnished
with pickled beets or
red cabbage.*

A 2 $^1/_2$ to 3-pound eye round roast
1   clove minced garlic
3   tablespoons grainy mustard
$^1/_2$ cup ketchup
$^1/_4$ cup red wine vinegar
3   tablespoons olive oil
$^1/_2$ cup red wine
$^1/_2$ cup water
1   cup crumbled ginger snaps

- Rub beef with garlic and mustard and place in baking dish. Add ketchup and vinegar.

- Let stand 4 to 12 hours, refrigerated, turning occasionally.

- Remove meat, reserving marinade.

- In a Dutch oven, sear drained beef in hot olive oil on all sides.

- Add marinade and wine and cook in oven, covered, at 350° for 1 $^1/_2$ hours.

- Remove roast. Add water to pan juices, then add crumbled ginger snaps and cook to thicken sauce.

- Slice meat (it will be crumbly) and arrange on serving platter, spooning gravy over the top.

GREEN ENCHILADAS

YIELD:

Serves 6

NOTES:

A great addition to your "busy day" entertaining file.

This takes only twenty minutes to prepare.

Add Avocado Rice (see page 146) and a salad and you have a quick dinner party.

¹/₂ cup chopped onions
1 clove garlic, minced
1 pound lean ground beef
1 teaspoon salt
¹/₂ pound Cheddar cheese, grated
1 cup medium hot salsa
1 (10 ¹/₂ ounce) can cream of chicken soup
1 (5 ounce) can evaporated milk
1 (4 ounce) can chopped green chilies
¹/₂ pound Monterey Jack cheese, grated
6 - 8 10-inch tortillas

- Sauté onions, garlic and beef together until beef loses its redness. Drain.

- Add salt, mix well and set aside to cool.

- When cool, add Cheddar cheese and salsa to meat mixture and stir to combine.

- In saucepan, blend soup, evaporated milk, chilies, and Monterey Jack cheese. Stir over medium heat until cheese is melted and mixture is smooth.

- Place ¹/₄ cup of meat mixture in center of each tortilla. Roll up and place seam side down in 9" x 13" baking pan.

- Pour chili-cheese sauce over the top. Bake at 350° for 30 minutes.

STEAK DIANE

YIELD:

Serves 4

NOTES:

Give this recipe a new twist by serving it with Orzo with Parmesan and Basil (see page 138) and Emerald Green Beans (see page 116).

4	beef tenderloin filets
1	medium onion, chopped
1	red onion, thinly sliced
6	large mushrooms, sliced
1	medium tomato, chopped
1	clove garlic, chopped
$1/4$	cup chopped parsley
	Dijon mustard
$1/4$	cup butter
$1/2$	cup red wine
1	teaspoon Worcestershire sauce
$1/2$	cup cognac, warmed

- Pound filets flat to about $1/2$ inch thick.

- Sauté onions, mushrooms, tomato and garlic in half of the butter until golden. Remove from heat and reserve, stirring in parsley.

- Spread mustard on both sides of filets.

- Sauté filets quickly in remaining butter, remove from pan.

- Add red wine and Worcestershire sauce to sauté pan.

- Return vegetables and meat to pan.

- Flame with warmed cognac and serve immediately.

GRILLED BEEF FAJITAS WITH GUACAMOLE

YIELD:
Serves 8

NOTES:

This is Tex-Mex finger food.

Guests can put together their own. Just put out warm tortillas, guacamole, cooked beef slices, and sauce with lots of napkins!

Tomato chili sauce can be made several days ahead.

1	(35 ounce) can Italian tomatoes, crushed
4	chili (or chipotle) peppers, seeded and diced
5	scallions, coarsely chopped
1	cup fresh cilantro
1	teaspoon salt
3	pounds boneless skirt steak or flank steak, trimmed of fat
1/4	cup olive oil
1	tablespoon grated lime rind
5	tablespoons fresh lime juice
2	teaspoons cumin
2	large cloves garlic, minced
2	large ripe avocados
8	tortillas

- Bring tomatoes with juice and chili peppers to a boil, reduce heat and simmer until thick, stirring with a wooden spoon for about 30 minutes.

- Add scallions and simmer 5 minutes more.

- Stir in cilantro and salt. Remove from heat. Cool.

- In a bowl, combine oil, 3 tablespoons lime juice, rind, cumin and garlic.

- Pour over meat and marinate in refrigerator at least 4 hours or overnight.

- Preheat grill or broiler, and broil meat 6 inches from heat 5 minutes per side.

- Cut meat into 1/4-inch strips, approximately 24.

- Mash avocados coarsely and add remaining lime juice.

- Heat tortillas on a griddle or skillet.

- Spoon 1/4 cup avocado mixture on tortilla and top with 3 - 4 strips of meat.

- Cover each tortilla with 1 or 2 tablespoons of tomato chili sauce.

- Fold up sides and roll like an egg-roll.

STUFFED VEAL ROLLS

YIELD:

Serves 6

NOTES:

Pine nuts, raisins and cheese bring new interest to this old favorite.

Accompany Veal Rolls with New Potatoes and Sour Cream (see page 132).

12   small thin slices prosciutto
12   small slices veal, pounded to $1/4$-inch thick
2   tablespoons pine nuts, toasted
1   cup parsley, chopped
3   tablespoons raisins
3   tablespoons freshly grated Parmesan cheese
   Salt and freshly ground pepper to taste
2   tablespoons olive oil
2   tablespoons butter
$1/2$ cup dry white wine

- Place a slice of prosciutto on each slice of veal.
- Combine pine nuts, parsley, raisins, cheese, salt and pepper.
- Place a spoonful of mixture in center of the prosciutto.
- Roll the veal jelly-roll fashion and tie with string.
- Melt oil and butter in a large skillet and brown the rolls.
- Add the wine, cover, and simmer for 10 - 15 minutes.
- Remove from heat, cut off strings and serve with pan juices.

VEAL MAROC

YIELD:
Serves 8

NOTES:
Quick and easy dinner party entrée.

Sherry, brown sugar and lemon juice produce a thick dark brown gravy.

Broiled tomatoes or Spiked Spinach (see page 119) would be a pretty accompaniment.

1 cup medium dry sherry
1 tablespoon dried oregano
1 teaspoon paprika
3 garlic cloves
1 cup packed brown sugar
1/4 cup fresh lemon juice
1 cup beef broth
1 cup water
1 carrot, sliced thin
1 large onion, roughly chopped
1 stalk celery, roughly chopped

- Blend all above ingredients in food processor.

3 pounds boneless veal shoulder or leg, cut into
   1 1/2-inch cubes
   Flour for dredging
1/4 cup olive oil

- Dredge veal in flour.
- Heat oil in Dutch oven, add veal and brown.
- Add all processed ingredients to browned meat.
- Cover and cook at 375° for 45 minutes or until tender.
- Serve over rice or noodles.

CURRIED VENISON

NOTES:

Curries don't have to be served with rice. This is delicious accompanied by spinach quickly sautéed in olive oil.

Don't forget the chutney.

5   tablespoons olive oil
4   tablespoons Madras curry powder
2   pounds venison stew, cut into 1 inch pieces
2   large onions, peeled and chopped
2   cloves garlic, minced
2   inches fresh ginger, grated
1   cup beef (or chicken) broth
1   tablespoon cinnamon
2   cups fresh or canned unsweetened coconut milk
8   small red potatoes, scrubbed clean
1   teaspoon sugar
    Salt to taste
    Mango chutney as an accompaniment

- Combine 1 $\frac{1}{2}$ tablespoons of oil with curry powder and coat the venison.

- Refrigerate overnight.

- In a large Dutch oven heat remaining oil and add onions, garlic and ginger.

- Cook, stirring frequently about five minutes.

- Add the venison and brown.

- Lower heat, stir in broth, cinnamon and coconut milk. Cook 15 minutes. If pan gets too dry, add $\frac{1}{4}$ cup water or broth.

- Add the potatoes, cover, and cook until potatoes are very tender.

- Add sugar. Salt to taste.

TOMATO CHUTNEY

YIELD:
Makes about 1 quart

NOTES:
A must when tomatoes are at their peak.
This is delicious with all sorts of meat.
For a quick hors d'œuvres, place chutney on top of cream cheese.

2 pounds ripe tomatoes, peeled and chopped
$^3/_4$ cup sugar
$^1/_2$ cup raisins
$^1/_2$ cup malt vinegar
2 tablespoons chili powder
2 tablespoons chopped fresh ginger
1 clove garlic, minced
$^1/_2$ pound onions, chopped
1 tablespoon cinnamon
3 red or green bell peppers, seeded and chopped
Dash of red pepper flakes (or cayenne)

- In a large saucepan, combine all ingredients.
- Cook slowly, stirring occasionally, 1 to 1 $^1/_2$ hours until thick.
- Pack into sterilized jars.

PEPPERED PEARS

YIELD:
Makes 16 pear quarters

NOTES:
Serve with platter of cold meats.
A delicious accompaniment to pâtés.
Sliced, it's wonderful inside a ham sandwich.

4 Bosc pears or other firm pears, peeled, halved and cored
2 teaspoons freshly ground black pepper
2 teaspoons sugar
$^1/_2$ cup dry white wine
1 $^1/_2$ tablespoons unsalted butter

- Preheat oven to 350°.
- Place pears, cut side down, in oven-proof baking dish.
- Sprinkle with pepper and sugar.
- Pour wine over pears.
- Dot with butter and cover.
- Bake until pears are fork-tender (30 - 45 minutes). Uncover and continue cooking 15 minutes.
- Remove from oven and let cool completely in liquid.
- Chill, covered, several hours.
- Quarter pears before serving.

BARBECUE SAUCE

YIELD:
Makes about 2 cups

NOTES:
Great for marinating and basting meat on the grill.

Double the recipe and store in the refrigerator. It keeps for ages.

$^1/_2$ cup oil
3 cloves garlic, chopped
$^1/_2$ cup wine vinegar
1 (6 ounce) can tomato sauce
2 tablespoons lemon juice
$^1/_4$ cup Worcestershire sauce
1 teaspoon oregano
  Salt and freshly ground pepper
1 (10 $^1/_2$ ounce) can beef bouillon
2 dashes hot pepper sauce

- Combine all ingredients in a saucepan and simmer 15 minutes.

MUSTARD SAUCE

YIELD:
3/4 cup

NOTES:
A grand sauce for ham.

4 tablespoons sugar
3 teaspoons dry mustard, or more to taste
1 teaspoon salt
1 tablespoon flour
1 egg, slightly beaten
5 tablespoons vinegar
$^1/_2$ cup half and half

- Combine dry ingredients in a saucepan. Add egg, vinegar and cream.
- Cook over low heat, stirring constantly, until thick. Cool.

Claude Howell (born 1915)
Mullet Haul, 1947
Oil on canvas
Gift of Mrs. Suzanne Ruffin Roth in memory of Virginia Bellamy Ruffin

As one of the South's most renowned artists,
Claude Howell has documented the people and environs
of coastal Carolina throughout his painting career.

Seafood

William Frerichs (1829~1905)
Falls in Cherokee County, NC, c. 1850-1865
Oil on canvas
Purchased by the Jessie N. Howell Memorial North Carolina Acquisitions Fund
and St. John's Museum of Art Memorial Acquisition Fund

Born in Belgium, William Frerichs immigrated to the United States. From
1855~1865 he lived in western North Carolina teaching and painting landscapes.

GARLIC AND LIME GRILLED SHRIMP

YIELD:

Serves 4

NOTES:

This marinade is excellent for grouper or other fish to be grilled.

¹/₄	cup fresh lime juice
¹/₄	cup olive oil
1	tablespoon chopped cilantro
1	small onion, minced
6	large garlic cloves, minced
1	large jalapeño pepper, seeded and minced
24	extra-large shrimp, peeled and deveined
4	bamboo skewers
1	cup jasmine rice, cooked

- In a small bowl, whisk together lime juice and olive oil until thoroughly blended. Stir in remaining ingredients, except shrimp and rice.

- Place shrimp in one layer in shallow pan. Pour marinade over and toss until coated. Let stand 1 - 2 hours at room temperature.

- Soak skewers in water for 30 minutes.

- Remove and drain shrimp, reserving marinade.

- Thread 6 shrimp on each skewer.

- Place marinade in small pan and heat over low heat and keep warm.

- Preheat grill or broiler on high 4 - 6 minutes. Then lower to medium.

- Place shrimp on grill and cook on one side for one minute. Turn and cook one minute more, or until shrimp are opaque. Place skewers on serving platter. Pour marinade over shrimp.

- Serve with jasmine rice.

PARMESAN FISH FILLETS

YIELD:

Serves 6

NOTES:

This is light, quick to prepare and utterly delicious.

Do not use non-fat sour cream.

8   ounces sour cream
$1/4$ cup freshly grated Parmesan cheese
$1/2$ teaspoon paprika
1   clove garlic, minced
6   fish fillets (flounder, trout, red snapper, or red bass)
1   teaspoon salt
1   cup toasted bread crumbs
2   ounces butter

- Combine sour cream, cheese, paprika and garlic.

- Place fish fillets in greased oven-proof serving dish and sprinkle with salt.

- Spread sour cream mixture on top. Scatter bread crumbs over and dot with butter.

- Bake at 350° for 30 minutes.

CRAB AND SHRIMP CASSEROLE

Yield:
Serves 8

Notes:
Served over thinly sliced boneless ham, it's sublime.

To vary, place ingredients in hollowed out red or yellow peppers, and bake as directed.

1   cup wild rice, cooked according to package directions
1   pound shrimp
1/2   pound fresh mushrooms, sliced
3   tablespoons butter
2   (13 ounce) cans artichoke hearts, drained and chopped
1   pound fresh crab meat, cleaned (see notes, page 6)
1/2   red bell pepper, chopped
1/2   cup chopped onion
1   cup chopped celery
1   cup mayonnaise
3/4   cup light cream
1   tablespoon Worcestershire sauce
    Salt and freshly ground pepper to taste

- Cook shrimp in boiling salted water until barely pink. Drain. Remove shells.

- Sauté mushrooms in butter until tender, about 5 minutes.

- Combine shrimp, mushrooms and all remaining ingredients.

- Pour into large ungreased casserole. May be covered and refrigerated at this point.

- Bake uncovered at 375° for 30 minutes, or until hot and bubbly.

BEST CRAB CAKES

YIELD:

Serves 4 as an entrée

NOTES:

These are spicy and moist.

Good with Pecan Tartar Sauce (see page 101) on the side.

1	pound fresh back-fin crab meat, cleaned (see notes, page 6)
1/2	teaspoon salt
1	teaspoon Dijon mustard
1/2	cup mayonnaise
2	teaspoons Worcestershire sauce
1 1/2	teaspoons melted butter
2	teaspoons parsley, finely chopped
	Dash of hot pepper sauce
2	tablespoons fine bread crumbs
1	egg yolk
1	teaspoon lemon juice
1	jalapeño pepper, seeds removed and finely chopped
1	clove garlic, minced
2	scallions, finely chopped

- Mix all ingredients together and shape into small cakes of desired size.

- Cook by either of the following methods:

  1. Sauté in butter until lightly browned, turning once.

  2. Preheat oven to 350°. Prepare baking pan with non-stick spray, and place cakes on pan. Bake for 10 minutes. Turn heat up to 450° and bake for 10 minutes until brown.

PECAN TARTAR SAUCE

YIELD:
Makes about ³/₄ cup

NOTES:
This is super on crab cakes or shrimp.
It is a new twist for any fish.

¹/₂ cup coarsely chopped pecans, toasted
¹/₂ cup mayonnaise
1 tablespoon cider vinegar
1 tablespoon minced parsley
1 teaspoon minced lemon zest
¹/₄ teaspoon salt
1 tablespoon minced pickles (or cornichons)
¹/₂ teaspoon dry mustard

- In a small bowl, combine all ingredients.
- Blend well and refrigerate until ready to use.

POISSONS AU VIN

YIELD:
Serves 4

NOTES:
When the flesh in the center of the fish is barely opaque, the fish is done.

2 tablespoons butter, melted
2 tomatoes, thinly sliced
1 cup toasted bread crumbs
   Salt and freshly ground pepper
4 fillets of fish (flounder or grouper)
²/₃ cup white port wine
2 tablespoons lemon juice
4 tablespoons butter
¹/₂ cup freshly grated Parmesan cheese

- Pour 2 tablespoons butter in bottom of oven-proof serving pan.
- Arrange tomatoes in the pan.
- Cover tomatoes with bread crumbs and season with salt and pepper.
- Place fish over crumbs.
- In a small saucepan, melt 4 tablespoons butter with white wine and lemon juice. Pour over fish.
- Cover with Parmesan cheese. Bake at 375° for 12 - 15 minutes for flounder, or at 425° for 10 - 12 minutes for grouper.

SEAFOOD MEDLEY

YIELD:

Serves 10

NOTES:

This is ambrosia for seafood lovers.

When poaching seafood keep liquid just below the boiling point.

1 ½   pounds salmon fillets
1   pound sea scallops
1   pound fresh lump crab meat, cleaned (see notes, page 6)
1 ½   pounds shrimp, peeled and cooked
½   pound butter (do not use margarine)
4   tablespoons flour
3   cups half and half
1 ½   teaspoons salt
¼   teaspoon pepper
1   tablespoon Worcestershire sauce
2   tablespoons capers
6   tablespoons freshly grated Parmesan cheese
2   teaspoons paprika
½   cup white wine
3   tablespoons sherry
1   cup toasted bread crumbs

- Poach salmon and scallops in wine for about ten minutes, or until salmon flakes with a fork and scallops are no longer translucent. Remove and cool.

- Flake salmon. Combine with shrimp, crab and scallops.

- For sauce: Melt butter in top of double boiler and gradually stir in flour.

- Add 1 ½ cups half and half and cook, stirring constantly until mixture begins to thicken.

- Gradually add remaining half and half and cook 5 minutes longer, stirring occasionally.

- Add salt, pepper, Worcestershire sauce, capers, 3 tablespoons Parmesan cheese, and enough paprika to make sauce pink.

- Remove from heat.

- Add all seafood to sauce and stir in sherry.

- Pour into a 3-quart buttered casserole.

- Top with bread crumbs mixed with remaining Parmesan cheese.

- Bake at 300 ° for 40 minutes.

CRAB IMPERIAL

YIELD:

Serves 10

NOTES:

When in a hurry substitute chopped pimientos for roasted red peppers.

1	green bell pepper, diced
2	red bell peppers, roasted, peeled, seeded, and diced
1	tablespoon English mustard
1	teaspoon salt
$1/2$	teaspoon white pepper
2	eggs
1	cup mayonnaise
2	pounds lump crab meat, cleaned (see notes, page 6)
	Paprika

- Mix together all ingredients except crab.

- Add crab and mix gently with fingers.

- Divide mixture into buttered ramekins or a 9" x 9" casserole.

- Sprinkle with paprika.

- Bake at 350° for 15 minutes or until hot .

- Serve hot or cold.

FRESH FROM THE SEA CASSEROLE

YIELD:
Serves 12

NOTES:
Serve with Nutty Wild Rice (see page 146).

Try serving it in pastry shells for a luncheon.

It will freeze.

If crab is unavailable, substitute lobster.

7   tablespoons butter
5   tablespoons flour
     Salt and freshly ground pepper to taste
     Cayenne pepper to taste
2   cups half and half
1/2 cup dry sherry
1   tablespoon Worcestershire sauce
2   tablespoons chopped fresh parsley
1   pound fresh mushrooms, sliced
2   (13 ounce) cans artichoke hearts, drained, rinsed, and halved
1   pound fresh backfin crab meat, cleaned (see notes, page 6)
1   pound fresh raw shrimp, peeled and deveined
1/2 cup freshly grated Parmesan cheese, grated
     Paprika

- Melt 4 1/2 tablespoons butter, and blend in flour, salt, pepper and cayenne.

- Add half and half, stirring constantly, until mixture thickens.

- Cool slightly and add sherry, Worcestershire sauce and parsley, stirring until blended.

- Sauté mushrooms in remaining 2 1/2 tablespoons butter until tender, about 5 minutes. Drain.

- Arrange artichokes along bottom of greased 9" x 13" baking dish in a single layer.

- Scatter shrimp and crab meat over artichokes and top with mushrooms.

- Pour cream sauce over the top and sprinkle with cheese and paprika.

- Bake at 350° for 30 - 40 minutes, or until center starts to bubble.

SHRIMP SKORPIOS

YIELD:

Serves 6

NOTES:

Try this with toasted focaccia.

Make sure shrimp are not overcooked.

5   tablespoons olive oil
4   cups chopped onions
1 ½   tablespoons dry mustard
6   tablespoons fresh dill (or 3 tablespoons dried)
1   tablespoon sugar
    Salt and freshly ground pepper to taste
1 ½   (35 ounce) cans Italian plum tomatoes
2   pounds headless raw shrimp, shelled and deveined
½   pound feta cheese

- Heat olive oil in a large pot.

- Add onions, mustard, dill, sugar, salt and pepper.

- Sauté, stirring, until onions are tender.

- Add tomatoes and mash them down with a potato masher or wooden spoon.

- Over medium heat, cook gently 20 minutes (uncovered), or until most of the liquid has evaporated, stirring occasionally.

- In a large casserole, combine shrimp and sauce.

- Crumble cheese and sprinkle on top.

- Bake at 350° for 20 minutes or until shrimp are barely pink.

TORTE OF CRÊPES AND SHRIMP

YIELD:
Serves 6

NOTES:
This elegant offering can be expedited by preparing crêpes several days ahead, and freezing them with plastic wrap between crêpes. Thaw for 1 - 2 hours and proceed with recipe.

CRÊPES:

1 cup flour
3 large eggs
1 cup milk
4 tablespoons chopped fresh cilantro, parsley, or basil
   Salt to taste
1/2 teaspoon white pepper

- Place flour in bowl, and make a well in the center.
- Crack the eggs into the well and beat them until flour is all absorbed. Slowly pour in milk, stirring constantly.
- Add herbs and seasonings to the batter.
- Let it rest in refrigerator at least one hour.
- Make the crêpes in a skillet or a crêpe maker so that crêpes fit a 9-inch cake pan.

FILLING:

1 sweet onion, chopped
1 clove garlic, chopped
2 tablespoons olive oil
2 large eggs
8 ounces Monterey Jack cheese, cut in chunks
6 ounces sour cream
1 1/2 pounds shrimp, cooked and peeled
   Salt to taste
1/2 teaspoon white pepper

- Sauté onion and garlic in oil until soft.
- Place in food processor with eggs, cheese and sour cream. Process until smooth.
- Butter a nine-inch cake pan, and start layering as follows: 1 crêpe, cheese filling, and several shrimp, ending with a crêpe topped with cheese filling.
- Butter a piece of parchment paper and place on top of pile, gently pressing down to flatten the stack.
- Cover tightly with aluminum foil and bake at 350° for 30 to 40 minutes.
- Let cool, invert onto serving plate and cut into wedges like a pie.

FISH FLORENTINE

YIELD:
Serves 6

NOTES:
Lovely combination of flavors.
Serve with crusty French bread to absorb the sauce.

6 fish fillets (flounder or salmon)
1 ½ cups dry white wine
2 egg yolks
1 cup cream
1 tablespoon butter, room temperature
1 tablespoon flour
½ teaspoon dried basil and dill combined
1 tablespoon freshly grated nutmeg
1 cup freshly grated Parmesan cheese
Salt and freshly ground pepper
2 (10 ounce) packages frozen chopped spinach, cooked and drained

- Place fish in 9" x 13" oven-proof dish and cover with wine.
- Poach gently in a 350° oven 6 - 10 minutes.
- Drain well, reserving liquid stock in a saucepan.
- Combine yolks and cream in a bowl. Blend well.
- Thicken wine stock by slowly whisking in yolk mixture.
- Blend butter and flour and add to wine stock along with basil and dill, stirring over very low heat until thickened.
- Add nutmeg, lemon juice and cheese (reserving 3 tablespoons for final topping). Season with salt and pepper.
- Place well-drained spinach in bottom of greased 9" x 13" pan.
- Add ½ of wine and cheese mixture, then fish, followed by remaining wine and cheese.
- Sprinkle with Parmesan cheese and paprika.
- Bake at 350° for 20 minutes. Then place under broiler for 1 - 2 minutes until browned.

CRAB STUFFED POTATOES

YIELD:
Serves 8

NOTES:
This is obviously best with fresh lump or back-fin crab meat. If not available, however, frozen may be used.

4 medium Idaho potatoes, scrubbed clean
$1/2$ cup butter
$1/2$ cup half and half
1 teaspoon salt
4 teaspoons finely chopped scallions, green tops included
1 cup grated Monterey Jack cheese
$1/2$ pound fresh crab meat, cleaned (see notes, page 6)
Paprika for color

- Bake potatoes. Cut in half, and scoop out insides.

- Thoroughly mash potatoes with butter, cream, salt, pepper, onion and cheese. Cool slightly.

- Fold in crab meat and refill shells.

- Sprinkle with paprika. Potatoes may then be wrapped in foil and frozen if desired.

- Thaw, if frozen, and bake at 350° for 20 - 30 minutes.

BANKS CHANNEL COQUILLES

YIELD:

Serves 6

NOTES:

This can be made in a casserole dish and served over parsley-sprinkled rice, garnished with lemon slices.

$^1/_2$ pound bay scallops
6 tablespoons butter
$^3/_4$ cup white wine
6 tablespoons flour
2 cups milk, warmed
1 cup light cream, warmed
   Salt and freshly ground pepper
1 teaspoon Worcestershire sauce
1 tablespoon lemon juice
$^3/_4$ cup grated gruyère cheese
$^1/_4$ teaspoon dry mustard
$^1/_4$ teaspoon Dijon mustard
$^1/_2$ pound small shrimp, cooked
$^1/_2$ pound crabmeat, cleaned (see Notes, page 6)
   Freshly grated Parmesan cheese

- Poach scallops in 3 tablespoons butter with $^1/_4$ cup wine for 2 minutes.

- Remove scallops.

- Make cream sauce by mixing remaining butter and flour. Stir while cooking for 3 minutes. Add milk and cream. Stir until thickened. Slowly add $^1/_2$ cup wine. Continue stirring until smooth.

- Stir in all other ingredients except Parmesan cheese.

- Butter scallop shells or ramekins and fill with seafood mixture.

- Top with Parmesan cheese and heat in 350° oven about 20 minutes until bubbly. May be browned under broiler if desired.

PORTUGUESE FISH PIE

YIELD:
Serves 4

NOTES:
This is comfort food.
May be made early
in the day and baked
when needed.
Ideal for a Sunday
night supper.

2   cups mashed potatoes
1   tablespoon chopped fresh Italian parsley
$^1/_2$ red onion, chopped
2   cups cooked flaked white fish (such as grouper, flounder or catfish)
$^1/_4$ cup melted butter
$^1/_2$ cup milk
1   cup fresh bread crumbs
1   teaspoon salt
$^1/_2$ teaspoon freshly ground pepper

- Heat oven to 325°. Grease a deep pie pan or casserole. Spread half the potatoes over the bottom.

- Sprinkle potatoes with parsley and onion.

- Place fish on top.

- Pour half of the melted butter over the fish and add milk.

- Cover fish with remaining potatoes.

- Combine bread crumbs with rest of butter, adding salt and pepper.

- Spoon bread crumb mixture over potatoes and bake for about 35 minutes. Place under broiler for a minute or two to brown top.

SCALLOPS CONCASSÉES

YIELD:
Serves 4

NOTES:
Quick and appealing.
Serve over rice.

4	ripe plum tomatoes, peeled and seeded
2	tablespoons olive oil
2	teaspoons butter
1 ½	pounds small scallops (if large cut them in half)
	Freshly ground pepper to taste
4	tablespoons finely chopped shallots
1	tablespoon fresh thyme
1	tablespoon fresh lemon juice
¼	cup finely chopped parsley

- Cut tomatoes in half, then halves into ¼ inch cubes.

- Heat oil and butter over high heat in a large skillet.

- Add scallops and pepper, stirring until lightly browned, about 2 minutes.

- Sprinkle shallots, thyme and tomatoes evenly over scallops.

- Cook, stirring, for 2 minutes. Add lemon juice and cook, stirring, for another minute.

- Sprinkle with parsley. Stir well and serve.

OYSTER DRESSING

YIELD:
Serves 4 - 6

NOTES:
This is a holiday favorite for oyster lovers.

A side dish for turkey, it's great for ham or chicken, too.

1	pound package cornbread stuffing
4	ounces melted butter
2	large Granny Smith apples, chopped
2	large onions, chopped
1	quart shucked oysters with liquid, checked for shells

- Mix all ingredients and place in buttered casserole.

- Cover tightly with foil.

- Bake in a preheated oven at 350° for one hour.

MASONBORO SOUND SHRIMP

YIELD:
Serves 6

NOTES:
*For a variation
substitute 1 pound
crab meat for shrimp.*

1 pound shrimp, cooked and peeled
2 tablespoons butter
1 cup chopped red pepper
1 cup chopped yellow pepper
$^1/_2$ small red (or Vidalia) onion
1 cup cream
1 tablespoon Worcestershire
$^1/_2$ teaspoon dry mustard
1 teaspoon vinegar
1 teaspoon salt
$^1/_4$ teaspoon red pepper
1 tablespoon fresh chopped dill
1 cup fresh bread crumbs
3 tablespoons capers, drained & rinsed

- Melt butter. Add red and yellow peppers and onion. Simmer until tender.

- Add cream and seasonings. Cook until thickened.

- At serving time, mix with bread crumbs, capers and shrimp.

- Bake at 375° for 10 minutes or until hot.

Vegetables

Juan Logan (born 1946)
Bad Dog on a Chain Barking at Two Passersby, 1970
Acrylic and china marker on canvas
Gift of Juan and Geraldine Logan

A native Southerner, Juan Logan attended Clark College
in Atlanta and Howard University in Washington, DC,
where he studied art and became acquainted with other
African-American artists. He has gained a national reputation
through numerous exhibitions of his paintings and sculpture.

ARTICHOKES AND MUSHROOMS

$^1/_4$ cup butter
2 (9 ounce) packages frozen artichoke hearts
1 pound mushrooms, sliced
$^1/_4$ cup dry sherry
$^1/_4$ cup chicken stock
$^1/_4$ cup freshly grated Parmesan cheese
    Salt and freshly ground pepper
    Pinch of dried oregano

- Defrost artichokes by heating them in butter in a skillet over low heat.

- Add mushrooms when artichoke hearts are tender.

- Add the sherry and the chicken stock. Cook for 10 minutes, stirring occasionally, until mushrooms are done.

- Stir in cheese, salt and pepper. Continue stirring until cheese is absorbed.

- Stir in oregano and serve.

BAKED ASPARAGUS

1 pound asparagus, stems trimmed
2 tablespoons butter
$^1/_2$ pound mushrooms, sliced
4 hard-cooked eggs, sliced
2 slices bread, toasted and ground into crumbs
    Freshly grated Parmesan cheese

- Steam asparagus until barely cooked.

- Sauté mushrooms in butter until liquid is released.

- In a buttered casserole or gratin dish, layer asparagus, eggs, mushrooms with liquid, and bread crumbs.

- Sprinkle top generously with cheese and bake at 325° for 1 hour.

EMERALD GREEN BEANS

YIELD:
Serves 6 - 8

NOTES:
*A fresh, colorful
accompaniment
to any main dish.
This is one of our
very favorites.*

2 pounds green beans, tips removed
4 tablespoons butter
2 ½ teaspoons grated fresh ginger
¾ cup walnuts, chopped
½ cup golden raisins
4 tablespoons fresh lemon juice
  Salt and freshly ground pepper

- Cook green beans in boiling salted water until barely tender, but still crisp, about 5 minutes.

- Drain and drop in cold water to cool. Remove from water and set aside.

- Melt butter in large skillet over medium high heat.

- Add ginger, nuts and raisins. Cook, stirring constantly, 2 - 3 minutes.

- Add beans and lemon juice, lower heat, and cook uncovered until beans are reheated.

- Season with salt and pepper to taste.

CAULIFLOWER SUPREME

YIELD:
Serves 8

NOTES:
This is rich and wonderful for a winter buffet.

1 head cauliflower
$^1/_2$ cup mayonnaise
1 $^1/_2$ tablespoons prepared mustard
4 slices bacon, cooked and crumbled
$^1/_2$ cup grated sharp cheddar cheese
Salt and freshly ground pepper

- Cook cauliflower, covered, until crispy tender in small amount of water.
- Break up into flowerets and place in buttered casserole.
- Combine mayonnaise, mustard and salt and pepper to taste. Pour over cauliflower.
- Sprinkle bacon and cheese over mayonnaise topping.
- Bake at 350° for 15 minutes, or until golden brown.

SHINDIG CARROTS

YIELD:
Serves 6

NOTES:
We tend to forget how good carrots are.

Inexpensive and can be treated elegantly.

8   carrots, peeled and julienned
2   tablespoons grated onion
2   tablespoons prepared horseradish
$1/2$ cup mayonnaise
$1/2$ teaspoon salt
$1/4$ teaspoon freshly ground pepper
1   tablespoon melted butter
$1/2$ cup fine bread (or cracker) crumbs
     Paprika

- In a saucepan, cover carrots with water and cook until tender.

- Drain, reserving cooking liquid.

- Plunge carrots into ice water to stop cooking process.

- Drain and place carrots in a greased shallow baking dish.

- Mix $1/4$ cup cooking liquid with onion, horseradish, mayonnaise, salt and pepper.

- Pour sauce over carrots.

- Combine butter and crumbs. Sprinkle on top.

- Dust generously with paprika. Bake uncovered at 375° for 15 - 20 minutes.

SPIKED SPINACH

YIELD:

Serves 6

NOTES:

This may be assembled in advance. Baking can take place while guests are having appetizers.

3   (10 ounce) packages frozen chopped spinach, cooked and drained
4   eggs, beaten
4   tablespoons grated onion
1   cup milk
8   ounces melted butter
$3/4$ cups Feta cheese
$3/4$ cups freshly grated Parmesan cheese
1   ounce brandy (or pernod)
    Salt and freshly ground pepper to taste

- Mix all ingredients.
- Pour into a greased 1 $1/2$ quart casserole.
- Bake at 350° for 40 - 45 minutes.

ALL YEAR-ROUND ZUCCHINI

YIELD:
Serves 6

NOTES:
A dressy treatment of a standby vegetable.
You don't even have to cook the zucchini!

6   small zucchini, cut into 1-inch cubes
2   tablespoons butter
2   tablespoons flour
1 1/2   cups milk
1   cup grated sharp cheddar cheese
1   teaspoon salt
1/4   teaspoon freshly ground pepper
1/4   cup chopped almonds, toasted
1/2   cup buttered bread crumbs
4   slices crisp bacon, crumbled

- Prepare zucchini by cutting in quarters lengthwise, then across into cubes.

- Place evenly in a greased casserole.

- In a saucepan melt butter, add flour, stirring until a smooth paste. Still stirring, gradually add milk, cook over medium heat until thickened and smooth.

- Add cheese, salt and pepper, stirring until cheese is melted.

- Sprinkle zucchini with almonds. Then pour on sauce. Sprinkle top with crumbs and bacon.

- Bake at 350° for about 30 minutes until cheese is golden and bubbly.

CAROLINA COLLARDS

YIELD:

Serves 6 with Corn Meal Dumplings

NOTES:

A true Carolina Coast treat!

1 bunch collard greens, about 1 $\frac{3}{4}$ pounds
1 pound mustard greens
6 strips thick bacon
1 large onion, chopped
1 red bell pepper, chopped
Equal amounts of white wine and water
Red pepper flakes, optional

- Rinse greens in water to remove sand and drain.

- Remove tough stems, and coarsely chop greens.

- In a large stock pot, render bacon slices until crisp.

- Place half the greens, half the onion, and half the bell pepper layered in the pot and repeat with remaining half.

- Pour in equal parts of wine and water to cover vegetables, adding red pepper flakes if desired.

- Cover and cook over medium heat until tender (about 3 hours).

CORN MEAL DUMPLINGS:

$\frac{1}{4}$ cup solid white shortening
2 cups corn meal
$\frac{1}{2}$ cup flour
$\frac{1}{2}$ teaspoon baking powder
1 teaspoon salt
Water

- Blend all ingredients except water.

- Add just enough water to hold dry ingredients together.

- Roll about $\frac{1}{4}$ cup of dough into a ball, then flatten with your palm until it's about $\frac{1}{2}$ to 1-inch thick.

- At end of collard cooking time, place cakes on top of greens.

- Simmer a few minutes, then spoon a few collard pieces and juice on top of each cake.

- Cook about 15 minutes until heated through.

COLD VEGETABLE MEDLEY

YIELD:
Serves 8

NOTES:
This colorful combination is best displayed in a glass bowl.

A bright accompaniment to broiled meat or fish.

1   pound broccoli flowerets
3   tablespoons olive oil
8   ounces frozen corn, thawed
1   clove garlic, minced
1/2   cup diced red bell pepper
1/2   teaspoon cumin
2   scallions sliced thin, including green part
1   pint cherry tomatoes, sliced in half
    Juice of one large lemon
    Salt and freshly ground pepper

- Blanch the broccoli and reserve.

- Heat oil in large skillet or Dutch oven.

- Cook the corn, garlic, red pepper and cumin in the hot oil for 2 minutes, stirring.

- Add the scallions and cherry tomatoes and cook, stirring for 1 minute.

- Stir in lemon juice, salt and pepper to taste.

- Transfer to a serving dish and let it cool to room temperature.

- May be made one day ahead and refrigerated, covered, overnight.

- Before serving, add broccoli and toss.

COASTAL CAULIFLOWER

YIELD:
Serves 8

NOTES:
This is a favorite old Southern recipe.

It is equally good made with broccoli.

This recipe is delicious using cheddar, swiss or dilled havarti cheese.

1   cauliflower head, broken into flowerets
1   teaspoon salt
2   cups bread crumbs, $^1/_2$ cup reserved for top
1   medium onion, chopped
2   cups grated cheese
1   tablespoon butter, melted
1   tablespoon flour
1   cup milk
2   whole eggs, beaten

- In a saucepan, put one-inch of water with salt and bring to a boil.

- Add cauliflower and cook, covered, until almost tender (about 10 minutes), lifting the cover 2 or 3 times to permit steam to escape.

- Remove from pan and drain.

- Butter a 9" x 13" baking pan, and layer the cauliflower, crumbs, onion and cheese. Repeat until used.

- Mix butter and flour, adding milk and eggs. Stir until smooth. Pour over casserole. Sprinkle reserved bread crumbs on top.

- Bake at 375° for 20 minutes.

BROCCOLI FRITTATTA

YIELD:
Serves 6

NOTES:
This is also very successful made with spinach.

6   eggs, unbeaten
2   pounds small curd cottage cheese
6   tablespoons flour
$1/2$ pound Havarti cheese with dill, cut in small cubes
2   (10 ounces) packages frozen chopped broccoli, thawed
$1/2$ pound butter, melted
4   scallions, chopped
1   teaspoon salt

- Have all ingredients at room temperature.
- Combine all ingredients.
- Stir until well blended.
- Pour mixture into a 9" x 13" greased baking dish.
- Bake at 350° for one hour or until set. Let stand 10 minutes before serving.

WHITE EGGPLANT

YIELD:
Serves 8 - 10

NOTES:
If white eggplant is unavailable, use purple.
Just soak slices in salt water before sautéing.
A delicious, filling casserole for a casual supper.

2   medium white eggplants
2   tablespoons olive oil
1   (16 ounce) can crushed tomatoes
1   clove garlic, minced
1   pound salami, sliced
$1/2$ pound freshly grated Parmesan cheese
8   ounces fresh Mozzarella cheese, sliced

- Slice eggplant $1/4$-inch thick.
- Pat dry and sauté in 1 tablespoon oil until soft.
- In another saucepan, cook tomatoes and garlic in 1 tablespoon oil.
- In a greased serving casserole, layer eggplant, salami, tomato sauce, Parmesan and Mozzarella. Repeat until full.
- Bake at 350° for 25 minutes, or until cheese is melted.

CRUSTLESS SPINACH PIE

YIELD:
Serves 8 - 10

NOTES:
This is a rich but simple side dish. Great with grilled fish or chicken.

1 cup flour
1 teaspoon salt
1 teaspoon baking powder
2 beaten eggs
$1/4$ pound melted butter
1 cup milk
$1/2$ cup chopped onion
$1/2$ pound sharp Cheddar cheese, grated
$1/2$ pound Swiss cheese, grated
3 (10 ounce) packages frozen chopped spinach, thawed and drained

- In a large bowl, mix flour, salt and baking powder.

- Add eggs, butter and milk.

- Blend in remaining ingredients.

- Lightly grease a 9" x 13" baking dish. Pour in spinach mixture and bake at 350° for 30 to 35 minutes. Cool 15 minutes before serving.

MOUSSAKA

YIELD:
Serves 8 - 12

NOTES:
This is probably the most popular Greek main dish.

It is indeed well worth the time to prepare.

To freeze casserole without tying up your dish for weeks, try this tip. Line casserole with heavy duty foil before filling it. Then freeze filled casserole completely, lift out frozen contents by the foil lining. Wrap the frozen food in more foil, put it back in the freezer, and put your empty casserole back in the cupboard. When ready to thaw, unwrap frozen contents, and put back in the same casserole for reheating and serving.

EGGPLANT:

2	medium eggplants, sliced crosswise into $1/2$" slices
4	large potatoes, sliced crosswise into $1/4$" slices
	Salt
	Olive oil
$1/2$	cup freshly grated Parmesan cheese

- Sprinkle eggplant slices lightly with salt. Let stand 20 minutes to leach out bitterness.

- Drain eggplant and pat dry with paper towels.

- Fry eggplant and potato slices in oil until golden brown, or brush with oil and broil on foil-lined cookie sheet until brown and tender, turning once.

MEAT SAUCE:

1	onion, chopped
2	cloves garlic, minced
2	tablespoons olive oil
1 $1/2$	pounds ground lamb (or lean ground beef)
$1/2$	cup red wine
$1/2$	teaspoon cinnamon
$1/2$	cup chopped parsley
	Salt and freshly ground pepper
3	ounces tomato paste
	Pinch of sugar
	Pinch of freshly ground nutmeg

- Sauté onions and garlic in olive oil until soft. Add meat and cook until it loses its redness, breaking up lumps.

- Add remaining ingredients and simmer about five minutes. Set aside and cool so that flavors may blend.

CREAM SAUCE:

3/4 cup butter
3/4 cup flour
 6   cups hot milk
 6   eggs
1/8 teaspoon nutmeg
     Salt and white pepper to taste
1/4 cup freshly grated Parmesan cheese

- In a 4-quart saucepan melt butter and combine with flour. Cook for 2 minutes, stirring constantly.

- Gradually add hot milk, continuing to stir until smooth. Remove from heat.

- In a blender or food processor, beat eggs until frothy. With machine running, add 2 cups of hot mixture to eggs and beat well.

- Slowly return contents of blender to saucepan , stirring constantly until mixture is thickened. Stir in nutmeg, salt, pepper and cheese. Set aside.

TO ASSEMBLE:

- Place half of the eggplant and potato slices in a well-greased 9" x 13" baking dish. Sprinkle with half of the cheese. Spread half of the meat mixture evenly over vegetables.

- Repeat with remaining eggplant, potato, cheese and meat mixture.

- Pour cream sauce evenly over the top of the casserole.

- Bake at 350° for 1 hour or until top is golden and puffed. Cool for 20 minutes before cutting.

VIDALIA ONION CASSEROLE

YIELD:
Serves 10

NOTES:
This is wonderfully rich.

May accompany broiled fish or chicken with a light vinaigrette salad.

8   medium Vidalia onions, chopped
4   ounces butter, melted
2   eggs
1   (12 ounce) can evaporated milk
1   cup grated Parmesan cheese
    Salt and freshly ground pepper to taste
8   ounces Monterey Jack cheese, shredded

- In a non-stick saucepan, cook onions with $1/2$ cup water until tender.

- Pour hot onions over butter in shallow casserole.

- Mix together eggs, milk, Parmesan cheese, salt, pepper and half the Monterey Jack cheese.

- Pour sauce over onions, and sprinkle with remaining Monterey Jack cheese on top.

- Bake at 350° for 30 minutes.

GOOD LUCK PEAS

YIELD:

Serves 6

NOTES:

Southern tradition dictates that on New Year's Day, you eat Carolina Collards (see page 121) for money, pork for love and peas for luck!

12   ounces fresh black-eyed peas
3   ham slices, cut into small pieces
1   large onion, diced
1   red pepper, diced
1   yellow pepper, diced
1   (6 $\frac{1}{2}$ ounce) jar pitted green olives, drained
1   teaspoon thyme
1   teaspoon oregano
     Juice of one lemon
8   scallions, chopped

• Rinse and pick over peas in a colander.

• In a stockpot, bring peas to boil in 7 cups water for 10 minutes.

• Remove from heat and cover for one hour.

• Drain off soaking water.

• To cook, combine all ingredients except scallions and simmer in 2 cups water, covered, until peas are tender. Add more water if necessary.

• Add scallions as garnish.

BEST-EVER BEANS

YIELD:
Serves 8

NOTES:
Absolutely splendid to accompany barbecued ribs!

1   pound smoked bacon, diced
1   cup onion, chopped
$^{1}/_{2}$ pound ground beef
$^{1}/_{2}$ cup ketchup
1   teaspoon salt
3   tablespoons grainy mustard
4   teaspoons cider vinegar or more to taste
$^{3}/_{4}$ cup packed light brown sugar
1   (30 ounce) can pork and beans
1   (15 ounce) can garbanzo beans (chick peas), drained
1   (15 ounce) can kidney beans, (drained)
1   (10 ounce) package frozen baby lima beans, thawed

- In a skillet cook bacon, add onion, then beef, draining off excess fat.

- Stir in ketchup, salt, mustard and vinegar.

- Combine all ingredients in a large casserole.

- Cover and bake 40 minutes at 350°.

BLACK BEAN CASSEROLE

YIELD:
Serves 10

NOTES:
A soul-satisfying treat for a winter's evening.

1 tablespoon oil
1 medium onion, chopped
1 clove garlic, minced
2 (15 ounce) cans black beans, drained
1 (10 ounce) can tomatoes with green chilies
1 (4 ounce) can diced mild chilies
2 tablespoons fresh cilantro chopped
  Dash red pepper flakes
  Salt and freshly ground pepper to taste
9 corn tortillas, each cut into 6 sections
1 1/2 cups Mozzarella cheese, shredded
1/2 cup Cheddar cheese, shredded

- In a saucepan, sauté onion and garlic in oil.

- Add beans, tomatoes, chilies, cilantro, pepper flakes, and salt and pepper. Simmer 10 minutes.

- In a 2-quart buttered casserole, layer 1/3 tortillas, 1/3 beans, and 1/3 cheese. Continue layering, and end with cheeses.

- Cover and bake at 375° for 20 minutes.

- Uncover and bake 15 minutes longer until cheese is browned.

POTATO CASSEROLE

6 medium white potatoes, scrubbed clean
$^1/_2$ cup butter
1 (10 $^3/_4$ ounce) can cream of chicken soup
$^1/_2$ cup green onions, chopped, including tops
2 cups sour cream
1 cup grated Cheddar cheese

- Cook potatoes with skins on until just tender.
- Coarsely chop potatoes in food processor or potato masher.
- Melt butter and combine with soup. Stir into potatoes.
- Add remaining ingredients and place in 2 $^1/_2$-quart buttered baking dish.
- Bake at 350° for 45 minutes. Let stand for 15 minutes before serving.

NEW POTATOES IN SOUR CREAM

4 tablespoons butter, melted
6 small red potatoes, scrubbed clean
$^1/_8$ teaspoon white pepper
$^1/_2$ teaspoon salt
$^1/_3$ cup sour cream
1 tablespoon chives
4 slices bacon, cooked crisp and crumbled

- Slice unpeeled red potatoes
- In a saucepan, add potatoes, salt and pepper to melted butter. Cook, covered, on low heat until tender for 10 - 20 minutes, stirring occasionally.
- Drain, if necessary, and add sour cream, chives and bacon.
- Heat for one minute more. Do not boil or sour cream will curdle.

GOLDEN SCALLOPED POTATOES

YIELD:

Serves 6

NOTES:

This is a hearty variation on scalloped potatoes.

Grits will cook as casserole bakes.

Julienne refers to vegetables sliced into thin, matchstick strips.

5 medium potatoes, thinly sliced
1 cup yellow corn grits
1 onion, thinly sliced
1/3 cup whole wheat flour (or white flour)
 Salt and freshly ground pepper
1/3 cup butter
2 cups Cheddar cheese, grated
1/2 red bell pepper, julienned
6 cups milk

- Partially cook potato slices in boiling water for 5 - 8 minutes. Drain.

- In a buttered 9" x 13" casserole, layer potatoes, grits, onion, flour, salt and pepper. Dot with butter and sprinkle with cheese. Repeat layers, ending with cheese. Arrange red pepper strips on top.

- Pour in milk until it covers top layer. Bake at 350° for about one hour, or until milk is absorbed and top is golden brown.

BOURBON SWEET POTATOES

YIELD:
Serves 8 - 10

NOTES:
A great companion for pork.

4 pounds sweet potatoes, scrubbed clean
³/₄ cup orange juice
1 cup brown sugar
4 tablespoons butter, melted
¹/₄ cup bourbon
¹/₄ cup orange liqueur

- Place potatoes in a large pot and cover with cold water.
- Bring to a boil, reduce heat and simmer 30 minutes or until tender. Cool and peel.
- Combine orange juice and brown sugar and stir.
- Place potatoes in mixer on slow speed. Add orange juice mixture, melted butter, bourbon and orange liqueur. Mix well.
- Pour into a 9" x 13" casserole.
- Sprinkle topping on potato mixture.
- Bake at 350° for 45 minutes to 1 hour.

TOPPING:

1 ¹/₂ cups pecans, chopped
¹/₂ stick butter, melted
1 cup brown sugar

- Mix topping ingredients.

Pasta, Grains & Rice

Francis Speight (1896-1989)
Tayloe House, 1971
Oil on canvas
Purchased with funding from the Jessie N. Howell Memorial North Carolina Acquisitions Fund,
Takeda Chemical Products, USA, Inc., and Tabitha Hutaff McEachern

A native of North Carolina, Francis Speight became nationally known as
a landscape painter and teacher at the Pennsylvania Academy of the Fine Arts
where he taught from 1925 until his retirement in 1961.

SESAME NOODLES

YIELD:
Serves 8

NOTES:
*This is the very best
of its kind.*
*Tangy Oriental
flavors blend to
perfection.*
*Must be made a day
ahead.*

2   tablespoons sesame oil (copper colored)
6   tablespoons sunflower oil
6   cloves garlic, finely chopped
2   tablespoons fresh ginger, finely chopped
6   tablespoons light brewed rice vinegar
6   tablespoons soy sauce
1   tablespoon Chinese hot oil (or chili oil)
3   tablespoons white sugar
1   pound vermicelli
6   scallions, diced

One day in advance:

• Heat sesame and sunflower oils in saucepan.

• Add garlic and ginger. Sauté until soft but not brown.

• Add vinegar, soy sauce, hot oil and sugar. Boil a few
  seconds.

• Cook vermicelli al dente. Rinse under cold water. Drain.

• Mix with sauce in large bowl until strands are well coated.

• Refrigerate.

• Next day, toss several times.

• Before serving, bring to room temperature, add scallions,
  and toss.

ORZO WITH PARMESAN AND BASIL

Yield:
Serves 6

Notes:
A flavorful addition to
a buffet table.

3 tablespoons unsalted butter
1 ½ cups orzo
3 cups chicken broth
½ cup freshly grated Parmesan cheese
¼ cup fresh basil, julienne (or 1 ½ teaspoons dried)
Salt and freshly ground pepper
Fresh basil leaves

- Melt butter in a large saucepan over medium heat.
- Add orzo and sauté 2 minutes.
- Add broth and bring to a boil.
- Reduce heat, cover and simmer until orzo is tender and liquid is absorbed (about 20 minutes).
- Stir in cheese and basil.
- Season to taste with salt and freshly ground pepper.
- Put in serving bowl and garnish with basil leaves.

GARDEN PASTA

YIELD:
Serves 8 generously

NOTES:
A very colorful dish.

2   tomatoes, diced
Juice of 1 lemon
8   ounces butter
4   cloves garlic, minced
16   ounces feta cheese
1 ½   pounds fettucini
1   pound fresh green beans, blanched and diced
1   red bell pepper, diced
1   yellow bell pepper, diced
2   carrots, grated

- Pour lemon juice over diced tomatoes in a bowl and refrigerate.

- In a saucepan, melt butter and sauté garlic for 3 - 5 minutes.

- Add feta cheese and cook, stirring, until it becomes a thick, soupy mixture.

- Boil fettucini in a large pot. Cook according to package directions. Drain.

- Put pasta in a large serving bowl, add all vegetables, toss with sauce, and serve hot with cooled tomatoes on top.

PROCESSOR PASTA

$^3/_4$ cup unbleached flour
1   egg, beaten
    Vegetable oil
    This ratio of flour to egg is based on one serving

- Put the flour into the food processor with the steel blade.

- Turn on machine and add egg slowly.

- Stop processing when the bowl looks like it's full of coarse sand, which, when pinched together, will be smooth and elastic, but not wet.

- If too dry, continue processing and add a little vegetable oil until it reaches the right consistency.

- Lightly flour a manual pasta machine and run through all seven settings, a handful at a time.

- Cut to desired size and allow to dry carefully placed on cookie sheets several hours before cooking.

- Boil ample water with one tablespoon oil added, and cook only 2-3 minutes.

- Serve with desired sauce.

NO-COOK SUN-DRIED TOMATO SAUCE

YIELD:
Serves 6

NOTES:
Serve over one pound of cooked bow-tie pasta.
Sauce may be made ahead.
A party pasta as well as family fare.

5   oil-packed sun-dried tomato halves
2   large firm tomatoes, peeled, seeded, and chopped
1/2   cup Niçoise olives, pitted
1/2   cup tightly packed fresh basil leaves (or 2 tablespoons dried)
1/3   cup pine nuts (or chopped walnuts)
1/3   cup freshly grated Parmesan cheese
2   cloves garlic, optional
1/2   cup virgin olive oil
    Salt and freshly ground pepper to taste

- Combine all ingredients in bowl of food processor.
- Pulse until blended to a chunky sauce.
- Add salt and pepper to taste.

PESTO SAUCE

YIELD:
Makes about 3/4 cup

NOTES:
Serve this immediately over pasta, chicken or fish.
It will freeze nicely.

1 1/4   cups packed basil leaves
3   cloves garlic, peeled
1/2   cup olive oil
1   teaspoon salt
3   tablespoons pine nuts (walnuts may be used if pine nuts are unavailable)
1   tablespoon butter, softened
1/2   cup freshly grated Parmesan cheese
2   tablespoons Romano cheese

- In a food processor with steel blade, process basil, garlic, oil, salt and nuts until smooth.
- Add butter and cheeses. Pulse on and off until blended.

ANGEL HAIR PASTA
WITH SPINACH AND PINE NUTS

YIELD:
Serves 8

NOTES:
Serve in decorative bowls with Italian bread, your dinner entrée is complete.

2   tablespoons butter
3/4 cup pine nuts
1/2 cup olive oil
4   very large garlic cloves (or 8 small), minced
3/4 teaspoon dried red pepper flakes
1   pound angel hair pasta
3   pounds fresh spinach
4   tablespoons butter
8   oil-packed sun-dried tomatoes, chopped
1/2 cup freshly grated Parmesan cheese

- Thoroughly wash spinach. Remove coarse stems.

- In a large skillet over medium heat, sauté pine nuts in 2 tablespoons butter until lightly golden. Remove pine nuts from pan.

- In same pan heat oil and sauté garlic and red pepper flakes for one minute. Remove from heat.

- Cook pasta al dente and drain. Place in large serving bowl.

- Reheat garlic oil, add spinach and toss over high heat for 2-3 minutes or until wilted. *Do not overcook.*

- Stir in butter and sun-dried tomatoes.

- Add spinach mixture, Parmesan cheese and pine nuts to pasta.

- Season with salt and pepper. Toss well and serve immediately.

FETTUCINI FLORENTINE WITH CHICKEN

YIELD:
Serves 4

NOTES:

*A general rule is
to use light sauces
for delicate pastas
like angel hair and
chunky, heavy sauces
for sturdy pastas such
as fettucini.*

8	tablespoons butter
1	onion, sliced
1/2	red bell pepper, julienned
1 1/2	teaspoons dried basil
2	garlic cloves, minced
1/2	teaspoon dried pepper flakes
1	pound boneless chicken breasts, cut in strips
2	(10 ounce) packages frozen chopped spinach, thawed and squeezed dry
	Salt and freshly ground pepper
12	ounces fettucini pasta
1	cup freshly grated Parmesan cheese
	Juice of one lemon

- Melt butter in large, heavy skillet over medium heat.

- Add onion, red bell pepper strips, basil, garlic and red pepper flakes, cooking until onion and red bell pepper are soft.

- Add chicken and sauté until cooked through, stirring frequently, about 10 minutes.

- Mix in spinach and season with salt and pepper.

- Cook and drain pasta according to package directions.

- Place warm cooked pasta in serving bowl, add chicken and spinach mixture, sprinkle with Parmesan and toss thoroughly.

- Drizzle with lemon juice and serve.

ARTICHOKE RAVIOLI

YIELD:
Serves 4-6

NOTES:
The tang of chèvre and the sweetness of artichokes make this a delightful combination. These may be served plain, or with our No-Cook Sun-Dried Tomato Sauce (see page 141) or Pesto Sauce (see page 141) for a main course.

1   (6 ounce) jar marinated artichoke hearts, drained
1/4   pound Chèvre cheese, room temperature
1   (4 ounce) package cream cheese, room temperature
2   scallions, coarsely chopped
30   won ton skins

- Put artichokes, Chèvre, cream cheese and scallions in food processor with steel blade. Process until smooth.

- Separate won ton skins.

- Place 1 heaping teaspoon artichoke mixture on fifteen skins.

- Brush edges of remaining skins with water.

- Cover filled skins with remaining won tons and press moistened edges to seal.

- Trim excess edges of filled skins with a sharp knife.

- Cook by either of the following methods:

  1. For ravioli: Drop into three quarts rapidly boiling water, trying not to crowd skins. Cook 3-5 minutes. Remove and drain on paper towels.

  2. For won tons: Heat 1/2 inch vegetable oil in skillet. Fry filled won tons in one layer 30 seconds on each side, or until golden brown. Drain on paper towels.

VEGETABLE LASAGNA

YIELD:
Serves 10 - 12

NOTES:
May be assembled a day ahead. Just bring to room temperature before baking.
This delights all pasta lovers.

³/₄ pound lasagna noodles
2   (10 ounce) packages frozen chopped spinach, thawed
2   tablespoons olive oil
1   onion, chopped
1   large clove garlic, minced
1   pound ricotta cheese
1   pound cottage cheese
¹/₃ pound freshly grated Romano (or Parmesan) cheese
3   eggs, beaten
    Salt and freshly ground pepper to taste
1 ¹/₂ quarts spaghetti sauce
1   medium zucchini, sliced thin
¹/₂ green pepper, sliced thin
³/₄ pound mozzarella cheese, grated

- Cook and drain noodles, following package directions.

- In a small skillet, heat oil and sauté onion and garlic.

- In a large mixing bowl, combine spinach, ricotta, cottage cheese, Romano (or Parmesan), onion, garlic and beaten eggs.

- Mix well and season with salt and pepper.

- Coat a greased 10" x 15" pan with sauce and assemble in order a layer of each of the following:
Noodles, ricotta-spinach mixture, slices of zucchini, green pepper, mozzarella and spaghetti sauce. Repeat layering process.

- Cover tightly with foil and bake at 350° for 45-60 minutes.

- Uncover and bake 15 minutes longer.

- Remove from oven and let stand 15 minutes before serving.

AVOCADO RICE

YIELD:
Serves 4 - 6

NOTES:
Does well as a side dish with lamb, beef or chicken - anything that isn't overpowered by sauce or gravy.

1   cup long grain rice
2 1/2   cups chicken broth
1   ripe avocado, peeled and cubed
Juice of 1/2 lemon
Chopped cilantro
Freshly ground pepper to taste

- Cook rice in broth 20 minutes.
- Drain and add remaining ingredients.
- Serve immediately.

NUTTY WILD RICE

YIELD:
Serves 8

NOTES:
This is indispensable for game, turkey, and all holiday cooking. Wonderful nutty flavor.

4   cups chicken stock
1   pound wild rice, carefully rinsed and drained
2   tablespoons butter
4   ounces pine nuts
2   onions, chopped
2   tablespoons parsley, chopped
2   tablespoons golden raisins
Salt and freshly ground pepper

- Bring chicken stock to a boil. Add rice.
- Cook until tender, about 1 hour, adding more liquid if needed. Drain.
- In saucepan melt butter, add pine nuts, sauté until golden brown and remove from pan.
- In same pan, sauté onions until limp.
- Add parsley and raisins. Cook 1 minute.
- Add onion mixture and pine nuts to cooked rice.
- Season with salt and pepper to taste.

MUSHROOM RISOTTO

YIELD:
Serves 6

NOTES:
Try substituting sake for the wine when using shiitake mushrooms, adding a teaspoon of minced fresh sage.

A different approach: Use dried wild mushrooms, soaked in warm water to cover for 30 minutes, reserving water. Remove tough stems, coarsely chop mushrooms and use the water in addition to the broth.

6 tablespoons olive oil
1 clove garlic, minced
1/4 cup chopped onion
5 cups chicken stock
2 cups arborio (short grain) rice
Salt and freshly ground pepper
1/2 cup dry vermouth, dry sherry or white wine
2 cups coarsely chopped fresh mushrooms
1/2 cup freshly grated Parmesan cheese

- In a large, non-stick saucepan, sauté garlic and onion in olive oil until wilted and translucent.

- In a separate saucepan bring stock to a simmer.

- Add rice, salt and pepper to onion mixture and stir to coat.

- Stir in wine, reduce heat and stir until fully absorbed.

- Add one cup of the hot stock to the rice and continue cooking over medium heat, stirring occasionally, until all the stock is absorbed.

- Continue stirring in stock by half cup increments as each stock addition gets absorbed.

- Keep heat adjusted so that the rice absorbs the stock without boiling away first.

- When you have added about half the stock, stir in the mushrooms. Continue in the same manner until all the stock is used.

- Turn off the heat. Stir in the Parmesan cheese. Taste and correct for seasonings. The risotto is ready when it is creamy in consistency outside and a little chewy inside each grain.

- Serve immediately.

INDONESIAN FRIED RICE

YIELD:
Serves 6

NOTES:
An exotic main dish, needing no other embellishment.

Indonesian Fried Rice is particularly delicious served with Cucumber Salad (see page 159) and sliced fruit.

2	cups white rice
3 1/2	cups chicken broth
1/2	cup cooking oil
2	cups onions, chopped
3	cloves garlic, minced
2	cups cooked chicken, cut into julienne strips
1 1/2	cups diced cooked ham
1 1/2	cups raw shrimp, peeled and deveined
1/2	teaspoon ground cumin
1/2	teaspoon dried ground red pepper
1	teaspoon ground coriander
2	tablespoons unsalted cashew nuts, chopped
4	tablespoons peanut butter

- Combine rice and broth in saucepan and bring to a boil.

- Cover and cook on low heat 20 minutes.

- Drain and spread on a cookie sheet or other flat surface to cool.

- Heat oil in a deep skillet and sauté onions 10 minutes.

- Add garlic and rice and sauté, stirring frequently.

- Stir in chicken, ham, shrimp, cumin, red pepper, coriander, cashew nuts and peanut butter.

- Cook over low heat 10 minutes or until shrimp have barely turned pink, stirring occasionally.

RIO GRANDE GRITS

YIELD:

Serves 6 - 8

NOTES:

A tangy variation of an old Southern staple.

For richer grits replace water with milk and prepare according to directions.

4	cups salted water, boiling
1	cup 5-minute grits
1 1/2	cups grated sharp cheddar cheese
8	tablespoons butter, melted
2	beaten eggs
1	(7 ounce) can chopped mild green chilies, drained
1	clove garlic, minced
1	tablespoon Worcestershire sauce
	Hot pepper sauce to taste

- Add grits to boiling water and cook, stirring, until thick.

- Mix remaining ingredients, and add to hot grits.

- Cook over medium heat until cheese is melted. Serve immediately.

Minnie Evans (1892~1987)
Untitled (face with crown of stars, surrounded by
angels, birds and white-winged creature), 1966
Crayon, graphite, oil and gold paint on paper
Gift of Mr. & Mrs. Bruce B. Cameron

Wilmington visionary artist Minnie Evans has gained
an international reputation for her unique creations. During
her 19 years as gatekeeper of Airlie Gardens, a private estate in
Wilmington, she produced thousands of artworks based on her
religious convictions and the fauna and flora surrounding her.

Salads

Clyde Jones (born1938)
Horse, c. 1989
Wood, paint, and mixed media
Gift of the 1990 fifth grade students of Brunswick,
New Hanover and Pender Counties

After a severe injury in 1979 working as a pulpwood logger,
Clyde Jones began passing time during his long convalescence
by cutting and assembling roots and stumps into animals. His
"critters," as he fondly refers to them, have been exhibited at
many museums including the High Museum in Atlanta, the
North Carolina Museum of Art and St. John's Museum of Art.

GREEK VILLAGE SALAD (Horiatiki Salata)

YIELD:

Serves 6

NOTES:

Everybody's favorite for lunch.

If your salad greens are wilted, soak them for an hour in fresh water with a few drops of vinegar and a sugar cube.

4	medium tomatoes, cut in wedges
1	medium cucumber, sliced diagonally
1	small green pepper, thinly sliced
4	scallions, thinly sliced
5	radishes, thinly sliced
1	head romaine lettuce, washed, dried and torn into pieces
20	black Greek olives (or Kalamata olives), pitted
$^1/_4$	pound feta cheese, crumbled (about $^1/_2$ cup)

- Combine all ingredients except cheese in a large shallow salad bowl. Toss to mix well.
- Pour dressing over salad and toss gently but thoroughly. Garnish with feta cheese.

GREEK DRESSING:

$^1/_2$	cup olive oil
$^1/_4$	cup red wine vinegar
1	tablespoon lemon juice
1	large clove garlic, minced
2	tablespoons chopped fresh parsley
$^1/_2$	teaspoon dried oregano
2	teaspoons dried dill weed (or 2 tablespoons chopped fresh)
$^1/_2$	teaspoon salt

- Place all ingredients in a covered container and shake well.

SPINACH SALAD AMANDINE

YIELD:
Serves 6 - 8

NOTES:
Perfect with grilled meat or fish.

Mandarin oranges may be tossed in for color contrast.

3 pounds fresh flat leaf spinach, washed carefully
5 ounces slivered almonds
1 (6 ounce) can pitted black olives
1/4 cup white wine vinegar
2 tablespoons dry vermouth
2 tablespoons soy sauce
1 teaspoon sugar
1 teaspoon dry mustard
1/2 teaspoon curry powder
   Salt and freshly ground pepper to taste
1 clove garlic, minced
2/3 cup olive oil

- Pat spinach dry with paper towels. Remove stems.

- Lightly toast the almonds in a 350° oven.

- Drain the olives. If they are large, cut them in half.

- Put spinach, almonds, and olives in a serving bowl, and set aside.

- Combine remaining ingredients except for oil in a blender or food processor.

- Turn on processor and add the oil in a very slow, steady stream.

- Pour the dressing on the spinach and toss thoroughly.

ITALIAN WHITE SALAD

YIELD:
Serves 10

1   bunch Romaine lettuce, torn
1   bunch red leaf lettuce, torn
1   small red onion, thinly sliced
1   (13 ½ ounce) can artichoke hearts, drained, rinsed and sliced
1   (14 ounce) can hearts of palm, drained, rinsed and sliced
½   pound mushrooms, thinly sliced
1   (2 ounce) jar diced pimientos, drained
⅓   cup freshly grated Parmesan cheese
    Italian Dressing (see below)

- Place lettuce in bottom of serving bowl.
- Top with remaining ingredients, ending with cheese sprinkled on top.
- When ready to serve, pour ½ cup Italian dressing over, and toss.

ITALIAN DRESSING

YIELD:
1 cup

NOTES:
In the summer serve this dressing over sliced tomatoes and onions topped with fresh basil.

½   cup olive oil
¼   cup white wine vinegar
1   clove garlic, minced
½   teaspoon dry mustard
½   teaspoon basil
½   teaspoon oregano
¼   teaspoon rosemary
1   tablespoon parsley, minced
1   tablespoon capers

- Combine all ingredients in a covered jar.
- Shake to mix and chill to use as needed.

GRAPEFRUIT ROQUEFORT SALAD

YIELD:
Serves 6

NOTES:
An attractive combination of flavors and colors.

Squeeze lemon juice over avocado slices to keep them from turning brown.

2 heads of Boston lettuce
4 large ruby red grapefruit, peeled and separated into segments
3 ripe avocados, thinly sliced lengthwise
6 ounces Roquefort cheese
   Red onion rings, thinly sliced
   Vinaigrette dressing (see page 158)

- On 6 individual salad plates make a bed of Boston lettuce leaves.

- Arrange grapefruit and avocado slices in an alternating pinwheel fashion on each plate.

- Crumble Roquefort cheese and sprinkle in center of pinwheel.

- Top with onion rings, and drizzle with Vinaigrette Dressing.

SPINACH STRAWBERRY SALAD

YIELD:
Serves 4

NOTES:
The colors in the salad make it festive.

Wonderful in the spring when berries are best.

1 pound spinach, washed and torn into pieces
1 pint fresh strawberries, washed, hulled and halved
1 cup slivered almonds
2 tablespoons butter
   Poppy Seed Dressing (see below)

- Gently combine spinach and strawberries.

- Sauté almonds in butter until golden brown.

- Drain and set aside.

- Mix all ingredients and toss with $^1/_4$ cup Poppy Seed Dressing.

POPPY SEED DRESSING

YIELD:
1 $^3/_4$ cup

NOTES:
This dressing will keep, refrigerated, about one week.

$^1/_2$ cup sugar
2   teaspoons dry mustard
2   teaspoons grated onion
1   small clove garlic, minced (optional)
$^1/_3$ cup white vinegar
1   cup vegetable oil
1   tablespoon poppy seeds

- Combine sugar, mustard, onion and garlic.

- Place in blender and add vinegar.

- Gradually add oil, blending thoroughly.

- With blender running, add poppy seeds.

CLASSIC CAESAR DRESSING

YIELD:

1 ¹/₂ cups

NOTES:

Pour dressing over torn Romaine lettuce leaves, and toss with diced anchovy fillets, Parmesan cheese, and Croutons (see page 27).

A grilled boneless chicken breast cut into strips can be added for lunch.

1   egg
Juice of 1 lemon
4   medium cloves garlic, peeled
2   tablespoons freshly grated Parmesan cheese
4   anchovy fillets, lightly rinsed
Salt and freshly ground pepper
1   cup olive oil

- Put all ingredients but olive oil in food processor with steel blade.
- Let processor run for 30 seconds.
- While running, slowly pour in oil in a steady stream.

VINAIGRETTE

YIELD:

About 1 ¹/₂ cups dressing

NOTES:

Without a blender, this may be mixed in a covered jar and shaken vigorously.

¹/₂   cup sugar
1   teaspoon dry mustard
1   teaspoon paprika
1   teaspoon salt
1   teaspoon celery seed
1   small onion, grated
1   cup olive oil
¹/₄   cup wine vinegar

- Place dry ingredients, onions and vinegar in a blender bowl.
- Turn on motor at medium speed, pouring in oil slowly.

CUCUMBER SALAD

YIELD:

Serves 6

NOTES:

This is the perfect companion to spicy curries, broiled meats and fish.

Plain yogurt can be substituted for the sour cream.

5 cucumbers, peeled and thinly sliced
2 tablespoons sea salt (or Kosher salt)
1 red onion, thinly sliced
3 tablespoons chopped fresh dill
$^1/_2$ cup sour cream
2 tablespoons vinegar
   Freshly ground pepper

• Sprinkle cucumber slices with salt and let stand one hour.

• Rinse thoroughly in cold water.

• Place cucumber slices in a clean dish towel and squeeze dry.

• Place in serving bowl and toss with onion, dill, sour cream, vinegar and pepper.

MINTY PEA SALAD

YIELD:
Serves 6

NOTES:
A very refreshing salad.

1 ½ cups shelled fresh peas
8 ounces snow peas, trimmed and stringed
1 cup fresh mint leaves
¼ cup sour cream
¼ cup mayonnaise
8 slices crisp bacon, crumbled

- Boil fresh peas until barely tender (about 2 minutes).
- Separately cook snow peas until bright and crisp (about 30 - 60 seconds).
- Drain both peas and rinse in cold water. Set aside.
- Reserve a few mint leaves for garnish and finely chop the rest.
- Cut snow peas into julienne strips, reserving a few whole for garnish.
- In a serving bowl, combine peas and gently toss with mint.
- Mix sour cream and mayonnaise and fold into peas.
- Refrigerate, covered, until ready to serve.
- Sprinkle with bacon and garnish with reserved peas and mint.

FROZEN PICKLES

YIELD:
Serves 10

NOTES:
Crisp, cold and very good to have on hand.

16 (3-inch) cucumbers, sliced ⅛-inch thick (4 cups packed)
¾ pound yellow onions, sliced ⅛-inch thick (2 cups packed)
4 teaspoons salt
2 tablespoons water
¾ cup sugar
½ cup cider vinegar
1 teaspoon dried dill

- In a 2-quart non-aluminum bowl, mix cucumbers, onions, salt and water. Let stand 2 hours. Drain, but do not rinse.

- Return to bowl and add sugar, vinegar, and dill.

- Stir occasionally until sugar has dissolved and liquid covers vegetables.

- Pack in freezer containers and freeze. Defrost and refrigerate when ready to serve.

CRUNCHY BROCCOLI SALAD

YIELD:
Serves 4

NOTES:
The key here is not to overcook the broccoli.

Flavor combinations are interesting

1 bunch broccoli, broken into flowerets
3 hard-boiled eggs, chopped
3 ounces chopped green olives
1/4 cup green onions, chopped
1/4 teaspoon salt
1/4 teaspoon celery salt
1/4 teaspoon dry dill weed
2 tablespoons fresh lemon juice
1/4 cup mayonnaise
1/2 cup slivered almonds, toasted

- Blanch broccoli, uncovered, 3 - 5 minutes until barely tender.

- Plunge into ice water to stop cooking and set color. Drain and place in bowl.

- Add eggs, olives, onions, seasonings, and blend.

- Stir lemon juice into mayonnaise until incorporated.

- Stir in almonds, add to broccoli mixture, and chill.

PARTY ASPARAGUS SALAD

YIELD:
Serves 20

NOTES:
*This salad has great
eye appeal.
An interesting
combination of
textures.*

4	pounds fresh asparagus spears
1	cup olive oil
1/2	cup tarragon vinegar
3	tablespoons sweet pickle relish
1	(2 ounce) jar chopped pimientos, drained
1 1/2	tablespoons chopped fresh chives
1	teaspoon salt
	Freshly ground pepper
1	hard-boiled egg
	Tomatoes, peeled and sliced for garnish

- Cook asparagus, covered, in boiling salted water, 6 - 8 minutes.

- Plunge spears into ice water to stop cooking and set color.

- Combine next seven ingredients in a covered jar and shake to mix.

- Arrange asparagus in shallow serving platter and pour marinade over spears.

- Cover and chill overnight.

- When ready to serve arrange tomato slices around spears. Sieve or grate egg over top.

DELICIOUS PEAS

YIELD:

Serves 10

NOTES:

This is a vegetable lover's delight.

A last minute dish, since it's easy to have all ingredients on hand.

2 (14 ounce) cans artichoke bottoms, drained and rinsed

1 (14 ounce) can heart of palm, drained, rinsed and cut into $1/2$-inch slices

2 (10 ounce) packages frozen baby peas, thawed not cooked

$1/4$ cup mayonnaise

$1/4$ cup olive oil

2 tablespoons tarragon vinegar

Salt and freshly ground pepper to taste

Chopped parsley

- Arrange artichoke bottoms and hearts of palm along the bottom and sides of a serving dish.

- Mix thawed peas, mayonnaise, oil, vinegar, and salt and pepper together.

- Spoon over the other vegetables, garnish with parsley, and serve.

SAUERKRAUT SALAD

YIELD:

Serves 8-10

NOTES:

This interesting recipe tastes like a good three-bean salad!

It lasts for weeks in the refrigerator.

Even non-kraut eaters will love it.

1   cup diced onion
2   tablespoons milk
2   (16 ounce) cans sauerkraut, drained, rinsed and drained again
1   cup diced pimiento, drained
1   cup diced celery
1   cup chopped green bell pepper
$^{1}/_{2}$ teaspoon celery seed

- Soak diced onions in milk 15 minutes to remove harsh onion taste.

- Drain milk from onion.

- Place onion mixture and remaining ingredients in an earthenware or glass bowl. *Do not place in a metal bowl.*

- Pour sauce over vegetables. Refrigerate.

- Make at least a day ahead to let flavors blend.

SAUCE:

$^{1}/_{2}$ cup salad oil
$^{2}/_{3}$ cup white vinegar
$^{1}/_{2}$ cup water
$^{3}/_{4}$ cup sugar
$^{1}/_{2}$ teaspoon salt

- Combine all sauce ingredients and heat until sugar is dissolved, then cool.

ASPARAGUS SESAME

YIELD:
Serves 6

NOTES:
Green beans may be deliciously substituted.

2 pounds thin asparagus
1 teaspoon minced garlic
$^1/_2$ teaspoon salt
$^1/_2$ teaspoon white pepper
2 teaspoons Dijon mustard
1 $^1/_2$ tablespoons lemon juice
4 tablespoons dark sesame oil

- Cook fresh asparagus 3 - 5 minutes. Refresh under cold water and pat dry gently with paper towels.
- Blend remaining ingredients by shaking in a jar or whisking in a bowl.
- Pour over asparagus and serve.

BOUILLON ASPIC

YIELD:

Serves 8

NOTES:

Tomato juice or vegetable juice may be substituted for bouillon.

When making jellied salads, oil the mold with mayonnaise for a little extra flavor.

2   packages unflavored gelatin
2   (10 $\frac{1}{2}$ ounce) cans beef bouillon
    Water
$\frac{1}{2}$ onion, grated
4   ounces Roquefort, feta cheese or fresh chèvre
2   heaping tablespoons mayonnaise
1   tablespoon Worcestershire
    Dash hot red pepper sauce
1   (14 ounce) can artichoke hearts, drained and quartered
    Raw spinach and lettuce leaves

- Soak gelatin in 2 ounces water.

- Dilute bouillon with 1 $\frac{1}{2}$ soup cans of water and bring to a simmer.

- Add gelatin and stir until dissolved. Remove from heat.

- In a bowl, combine onion, cheese and mayonnaise. Add Worcestershire and pepper sauce. Mix until smooth.

- Oil a mold and pour in bouillon.

- Drop cheese mixture into liquid by heaping teaspoonfuls, scattering throughout mold.

- Place artichoke hearts in mixture, spacing evenly.

- Refrigerate until firm. (Allow a minimum of 3 hours.) Unmold and serve on a bed of spinach and lettuce leaves.

RUSSIAN BEET MOLD

YIELD:

Serves 8

NOTES:

Very colorful.

Especially zesty as an accompaniment to Poissons au Vin (see page 101) or Best Crab Cakes (see page 100).

1 (16 ounce) can julienned beets
1 envelope unflavored gelatin
$^1/_3$ cup red wine vinegar
3 tablespoons sugar
   One small onion, finely chopped
$^1/_2$ teaspoon salt
   Dash hot pepper sauce

- Drain beet juice into saucepan.

- Soften gelatin in beet juice and add vinegar, sugar, onion, salt and pepper sauce.

- Heat, stirring, until gelatin is dissolved.

- Add beets, and pour into 2 $^1/_2$-cup oiled mold.

- Chill to set. (Allow a minimum of 3 hours.) Unmold onto serving dish.

- Serve with Horseradish Sauce on the side.

HORSERADISH SAUCE:

3 tablespoons prepared horseradish
1 teaspoon onion juice
2 teaspoons white vinegar
$^1/_2$ teaspoon sugar
$^1/_2$ teaspoon dry mustard
1 teaspoon salt
$^1/_2$ cup mayonnaise
1 cup sour cream

- Thoroughly blend horseradish, onion juice, vinegar, sugar, mustard and salt.

- Add mayonnaise and sour cream. Keep refrigerated until ready to serve.

ROASTED PEPPER SALAD

YIELD:

Serves 6

NOTES:

A happy partner to any meat or fish.

Can be doubled for a larger group.

4   bell peppers, combination of red, yellow and orange
$1/4$ cup olive oil
2   tablespoons sherry vinegar
1   clove garlic, mashed
2   tablespoons capers, drained and rinsed
1   teaspoon paprika
    Salt and freshly ground pepper
2   tablespoons onions, finely chopped
$1/4$ cup parsley, chopped

- Roast peppers in a 375° oven for 17 minutes or until skins turn black.
- Turn and roast another 17 minutes.
- Put in a paper bag, twist top, and let steam until cool.
- Remove skin and seeds and cut into strips.
- Combine olive oil, vinegar, garlic, capers, paprika, salt and pepper.
- Arrange pepper strips in shallow dish, alternating colors.
- Sprinkle onions and parsley on top.
- Pour dressing over peppers and refrigerate.
- Return to room temperature before serving.

LENTIL SALAD

YIELD:
Serves 8

NOTES:
Great for picnics.
It is important to
remove a bay leaf
from any dish before
serving.

2 cups lentils
6 cloves
1 carrot
1 teaspoon salt
1 teaspoon dried oregano
2 cloves garlic, minced
1 bay leaf
$^1\!/_4$ cup balsamic (or red wine) vinegar
$^1\!/_4$ cup olive oil
$^1\!/_2$ teaspoon salt
1 $^1\!/_2$ tablespoons fresh basil, minced
2 cups cherry tomatoes, halved
$^1\!/_2$ cup blanched slivered almonds, toasted
$^1\!/_2$ cup chopped fresh parsley
$^1\!/_2$ cup crumbled feta cheese
$^1\!/_3$ cup thinly sliced green onions

- In a large saucepan, combine lentils with 1 quart water.
- Stick cloves into carrot. Add to lentils.
- Stir in 1 teaspoon salt, dried oregano, half the minced garlic and bay leaf.
- Cover and bring to a boil. Simmer 20 minutes.
- Drain lentils and discard carrot, cloves and bay leaf.
- Whisk together vinegar and olive oil. Add $^1\!/_2$ teaspoon salt, basil and the remaining garlic.
- Toss with lentils in a large serving bowl and cool.
- Toss in tomatoes, almonds, parsley, feta cheese and green onions.
- Cover and chill until ready to serve.

BLACK BEAN AND BELL PEPPER SALAD

YIELD:
Serves 12

NOTES:
*This is a good
substitute for
potato salad.
It's lighter but
filling, and has
no mayonnaise.*

*For a change, make it
with black-eyed peas.*

2   (16 ounce) cans black beans, rinsed and drained
2   cups cooked corn
2   red bell peppers, seeded and diced
1   yellow bell pepper, seeded and diced
1   orange bell pepper, seeded and diced
1   cup minced red (or Vidalia) onion
$^1/_2$ cup olive oil
$^1/_4$ cup Balsamic vinegar
     Salt and freshly ground pepper to taste
     Lettuce leaves

- Mix beans and corn with remaining ingredients except lettuce. Refrigerate.

- Before serving bring salad to room temperature and adjust seasonings. Serve on a bed of lettuce.

RED POTATO SALAD

YIELD:
Serves 6

NOTES:
When boiling any root vegetable such as potatoes start in cold water then bring to boil.

2 pounds small red potatoes, scrubbed clean
1 bunch scallions, sliced
3 hard cooked eggs, chopped
1/3 cup sliced celery
1/2 cup sliced radishes
1/2 pound bacon, cooked and drained
  Pecan-Basil Vinaigrette (see below)

- Boil potatoes until tender. Cool and cut into cubes.
- Add scallions, eggs, celery and radishes.
- Crumble bacon and sprinkle over potatoes.
- Toss 1/2 cup Pecan-Basil Vinaigrette with potatoes until coated. Add more Vinaigrette if needed.

PECAN-BASIL VINAIGRETTE

YIELD:
About 1 1/2 cups

NOTES:
Dressing can be stored, covered, in the refrigerator for a week.

1 tablespoon Dijon mustard
1/3 cup balsamic vinegar
1 cup basil leaves
  Salt and freshly ground pepper
1 cup olive oil
3/4 cup pecans

- Combine mustard, vinegar, basil and salt and pepper in food processor.
- With motor running, slowly add olive oil, scraping down bowl as necessary.
- Drop in pecans and pulse until chopped evenly.

172

CURRIED RICE SALAD

YIELD:
Serves 4 - 6

NOTES:
A zesty side dish.

2 ½   cups cooked rice
¾   cup roasted and salted peanuts
¾   cup frozen peas, thawed
1   medium onion, chopped
¼   cup vegetable oil
1   tablespoon curry powder
⅓   cup cider vinegar
2   tablespoons lemon juice
2   tablespoons honey
¾   cup raisins

- Combine rice, peanuts, peas and onion in serving bowl.
- Heat oil in small saucepan and add curry powder.
- Stir in vinegar, lemon juice, honey and raisins and simmer about 5 minutes or until raisins plump up.
- Pour dressing over rice and mix well. Chill.

ORANGE COUSCOUS SALAD

YIELD:
Serves 8

NOTES:
Colorful, light and refreshing.

For variety you can substitute blanched broccoli for green beans. Add just before serving.

1 1/2 cups couscous
1/2 teaspoon salt
2 cups boiling water
1 cup carrots, julienned and steamed
1 cup green beans, julienned and steamed
1 large red pepper, seeded and julienned
1/3 cup diced red onion
1/3 cup raisins
1/2 cup almonds, toasted and slivered

- Put couscous in salted boiling water, remove from heat and cover. Let stand until couscous absorbs all liquid. Uncover and cool.

- Add vegetables, raisins and almonds.

- Toss thoroughly with dressing.

DRESSING:

1/2 cup olive oil
4 tablespoons lemon juice
1/4 teaspoon cinnamon
3 tablespoons orange juice
4 tablespoons chopped parsley
1 tablespoon chopped fresh mint
  Cayenne pepper to taste

- Combine dressing ingredients.

SOUTH OF THE BORDER BLACK BEANS

YIELD:
Serves 8

NOTES:
This makes a complete meal with Bacon Cornbread (see page 217) and a glass of good red wine.

3   (15-ounce) cans black beans, drained
$^3/_4$ cup blanched slivered almonds, toasted
2   (11-ounce) cans Mexican corn, drained
1   cup fresh tomatoes, chopped
$^1/_2$ cup very thinly sliced red (or Vidalia) onions
1   red bell pepper, diced
1   yellow bell pepper, diced
$^1/_3$ cup chopped cilantro
    Salt and freshly ground pepper to taste
1   cup diced ripe avocado
    Chili Garlic Viniagrette (see below)

- Toss beans with chili garlic vinaigrette, almonds, corn, tomatoes, onions, peppers and cilantro.

- Season with salt and pepper to taste.

- Chill until ready to serve.

- Add avocado.

CHILI GARLIC VINAIGRETTE

YIELD:
Makes $^3/_4$ cup

NOTES:
You can use this viniagrette as a marinade.

$^1/_2$ cup Balsamic vinegar
$^1/_4$ cup olive oil
1   clove garlic, minced
1   teaspoon chili powder
$^1/_2$ teaspoon ground cumin

- Combine all ingredients in small mixing bowl. Whisk until thoroughly blended.

AVOCADO CRAB FLORENTINE

YIELD:

Serves 6

NOTES:

An attractive entrée.

The crabmeat mixture can be served in seeded, hollowed-out tomatoes.

Sprinkle avocado with lemon juice to keep from discoloring.

2 bunches scallions, chopped

2 garlic cloves, mashed

2 (10 ounce) packages frozen chopped spinach, cooked and drained

$1/4$ cup mayonnaise

1 pound fresh lump crab meat, cleaned (see notes, page 6)

3 ounces freshly grated Parmesan cheese

Dash of hot red pepper sauce

Salt and freshly ground pepper to taste

3 ripe avocados, cut in half lengthwise, seeds removed

1 bunch of red leaf lettuce

- Fold scallions, garlic and spinach into mayonnaise.

- Add crab meat, cheese, hot pepper sauce, salt, pepper and mix gently.

- Fill avocado halves and serve on a bed of lettuce.

CHICKEN AND FETA SALAD

YIELD:
Serves 4

NOTES:
A light, colorful pasta salad.

8 ounces bowtie pasta, cooked
2 cooked boneless, skinless chicken breasts, thinly sliced
4 artichoke hearts, quartered
$^1/_2$ cup black olives, sliced
1 tomato, sliced
6 thin slices red (or Vidalia) onion
$^1/_4$ pound feta cheese, crumbled
    Sun-Dried Tomato Vinaigrette (see below)

• Combine all ingredients and toss with $^3/_4$ cup Sun-Dried Tomato Vinaigrette.

SUN-DRIED TOMATO VINAIGRETTE

YIELD:
Makes about 1 $^1/_2$ cups

NOTES:
Any remaining vinaigrette can be saved for another time.
A good dressing for tomatoes and cucumbers.

12 oil-packed sun-dried tomatoes, drained
2 cloves garlic
1 tablespoon fresh basil
$^1/_4$ cup balsamic vinegar
    Salt and freshly ground pepper to taste
$^3/_4$ cup olive oil

• Purée all ingredients but oil in food processor.
• With machine running, gradually add $^1/_2$ cup oil to make a smooth sauce.
• If it is too thick add a portion of the remaining $^1/_4$ cup of oil until the Vinaigrette is of desired consistency.

CHICKEN COUSCOUS SALAD

YIELD:
Serves 14

NOTES:
This dish may be prepared a day ahead of serving.

12 chicken pieces, skinned and poached, reserving all liquid
2 (10 ounce) boxes couscous
2 tomatoes, chopped
6 green onions, chopped
2 (15 ounce) cans chick peas, rinsed and drained
1 red bell pepper, julienned
1 cup dried currants
1/2 cup chopped fresh parsley

- Bone chicken and cut meat in large chunks. Put in serving bowl.

- Follow instructions on couscous box, for the required amount of liquid.

- Bring broth to boil over medium high heat and add couscous, stirring.

- Cover, remove from heat and let stand until couscous absorbs all liquid. Uncover and cool. Transfer to bowl with chicken.

- Add tomatoes, green onions, chick peas, red pepper, currants and chopped parsley. Mix until well combined.

- Add dressing to couscous and toss to combine. Refrigerate.

DRESSING:

1/2 cup lemon juice
1/2 cup olive oil
1/2 teaspoon ground cumin
1/2 teaspoon curry powder
1/2 teaspoon minced garlic
    Cayenne pepper to taste
    Salt and freshly ground pepper

- Blend lemon juice, oil, cumin, curry powder, garlic and cayenne.

- Salt and pepper to taste.

SHRIMP-RICE SALAD

YIELD:
Serves 8

NOTES:
*Our testers agreed
that this is a recipe
that can substitute
yogurt for sour cream
with no loss of flavor.
A grand luncheon
dish!*

2   pounds medium shrimp, cooked and cleaned
2   cups cooked rice
$^1/_2$ cup seedless golden raisins
$^1/_2$ cup chopped dry roasted peanuts
1   teaspoon curry powder
1   teaspoon prepared horseradish
1   teaspoon fresh ginger, finely chopped
$^1/_2$ cup tomato sauce
1   cup sour cream
   Chopped parsley and chopped peanuts for garnish

- Combine shrimp, rice, raisins and peanuts in a bowl.

- Blend curry, horseradish, ginger, tomato sauce and sour cream in a separate bowl.

- Combine with shrimp mixture.

- Cover and chill for several hours to blend flavors.

- Serve garnished with chopped parsley and chopped peanuts.

GRILLED MUSTARD CHICKEN

YIELD:
Serves 4

NOTES:
Ideally, chicken should be served hot off the grill.
Easy and delicious.

$^{1}/_{3}$ cup butter
4 teaspoons Dijon mustard
4 teaspoons lemon juice
1 teaspoon garlic salt
2 teaspoons dried tarragon (or 4 teaspoons fresh)
$^{1}/_{2}$ teaspoon freshly ground pepper
4 chicken breasts, boned and skinned
   Mixed greens
   Vinaigrette (see page 158)

- Melt butter and mix in all ingredients except chicken.

- Coat each piece of chicken on each side with butter - herb mixture.

- Refrigerate 3 - 4 hours.

- Grill 3 - 4 minutes on each side, basting with remaining marinade.

- Slice chicken and place over mixed greens, with Vinaigrette on the side.

ORIENTAL BEEF SALAD

YIELD:
Serves 12

NOTES:
This zesty main course may be made ahead, chilled, and tossed with dressing just before serving.

A 4-pound London broil
1/3 cup soy sauce
1/3 cup dry sherry
1/3 cup oil
1 garlic clove, minced
1 bunch broccoli, cut into bite-sized flowerets
4 cups fresh asparagus sliced diagonally in 2-inch pieces
1/2 pound fresh Enoki mushrooms
1/2 pound cherry tomatoes, halved
6 scallions, white part only, cut into 2-inch pieces and quartered lengthwise
1/2 red bell pepper, julienne
1/2 yellow pepper, julienne
1 carrot, julienned into match-stick pieces
Toasted sesame seeds

- Marinate steak one hour in combined soy sauce, sherry, oil and garlic. Remove steak, reserving marinade.
- Blanch broccoli and asparagus 3 - 4 minutes (still crunchy).
- Heat marinade to a boil. Cool.
- Broil steak to desired doneness.
- Cool and slice thinly across grain.
- In a bowl, combine remaining vegetables and sesame seeds; add reserved marinade.
- Just before serving, toss beef slices in Ginger Sesame Dressing.
- Add all vegetables and toss again.
- Serve at room temperature.

GINGER SESAME DRESSING:

1/3 cup soy sauce
1/4 cup white vinegar
3 tablespoons sesame oil
1 1 1/2" piece of fresh ginger, peeled and grated
1 teaspoon sugar
Freshly ground white pepper

- Combine all ingredients for dressing.

CHICKEN MANGO SALAD

YIELD:
Serves 8

NOTES:
*This should be made a
day ahead to allow
the flavors to marry.*

*For an appetizer fill
pastry cups with this
salad.*

1   cup dry white wine
1   teaspoon salt
1   tablespoon black peppercorns
    Juice of one lemon
1   teaspoon fresh rosemary leaves
2   pounds chicken breasts, skinned and boned
1   ripe mango, chopped
1   ripe papaya, chopped (or 1 cup ripe cantaloupe, chopped)
1   bunch watercress leaves, chopped
    Green tops of one bunch of scallions, chopped
    Chutney Mayonnaise (see below)

- In a large saucepan, combine the wine, salt, peppercorns, lemon juice and rosemary.
- Add chicken and enough water to cover.
- Cover pan and bring to a boil.
- Remove pan from heat and allow chicken to cool in liquid for 45 minutes.
- Cut chicken into chunks and place in serving bowl.
- Add fruit, watercress and scallions.
- Toss with Chutney Mayonnaise until blended. Refrigerate.

CHUTNEY MAYONNAISE

YIELD:
1 ¹/₂ cups

NOTES:
*Chutney Mayonnaise
also is excellent with
shrimp, smoked
turkey, or country
ham.*

1   tablespoon olive oil
1   onion, finely chopped
2   tablespoons curry powder
1   cup mayonnaise
    Juice of 1 lime
4   ounces sour cream
2   tablespoons mango chutney

- In a skillet, heat oil, and add onion. Stir over low heat about 10 minutes or until onion is golden brown.
- Add curry and cook, stirring, about 2 minutes. Allow to cool.
- In a bowl, combine onion mixture with mayonnaise.
- Add lime juice, sour cream and chutney.

COLD LIME AND BASIL CHICKEN

YIELD:
Serves 4

NOTES:
Cold Lime and Basil Chicken must marinate in the refrigerator overnight. This marinade is especially good for grilling chicken!

3 cups chicken stock
4 chicken breasts
1 red bell pepper, julienne
   Salad greens

- In a large saucepan, bring the stock to a boil.
- Add chicken breasts in a single layer.
- Lower the heat, cover and simmer until done (juices run clear when pierced by a fork), about 15 minutes.
- Remove from heat and let chicken cool in the stock.
- Drain, saving stock for another use. Discard the skin and bones.
- Slice chicken into $1/2$-inch strips and place in a shallow glass dish.
- Pour marinade over chicken strips, cover and refrigerate overnight.
- Drain off the marinade and arrange the chicken on a bed of salad greens.
- Garnish with julienned red bell pepper slices.

MARINADE:
$1/2$ cup fresh lime juice (about 4 large limes)
2 large garlic cloves, peeled and crushed
2 tablespoons packed fresh basil leaves (or 1 tablespoon dried)
2 large shallots, minced
$1/2$ cup olive oil
$3/4$ teaspoon sugar
$1/2$ teaspoon salt
   Freshly ground pepper to taste

- In a small bowl, combine all marinade ingredients.

DUCK SALAD WITH GINGER DRESSING

YIELD:
Serves 6

NOTES:
Wonderful for leftover turkey.

2 cups cooked duck, cubed
1 cup crisp apples, peeled and cubed
1 cup orange slices, peeled
1/2 cup celery, finely diced
1 cup seedless grapes, sliced
1 small red onion, minced
1/4 cup chopped pecans
Ginger Dressing (see below)

- Combine all ingredients in a serving bowl.
- Toss with Ginger Dressing.

GINGER DRESSING

YIELD:
3 cups

1/2 cup onion, chopped
1/2 cup carrot, chopped
2 teaspoons celery seed
1 1/2 teaspoons, finely minced fresh ginger
1 1/4 cups olive oil
3/4 cup soy sauce
1/2 cup rice vinegar
1/4 cup lemon juice
1 1/2 teaspoons tomato paste
Salt and freshly ground pepper
Dash of hot pepper sauce

- Purée onion, carrot, celery seed and ginger in food processor.
- Add oil, soy sauce, rice vinegar, lemon juice and tomato paste, blending well.
- Season to taste with salt, pepper and hot sauce.

SMOKED TURKEY AND WILD RICE SALAD

YIELD:

Serves 4

NOTES:

*The smokiness in
the flavor adds to
the interest.*

$^1/_4$ cup dry sherry
$^1/_2$ cup mayonnaise
  1   cup cooked wild rice
$^1/_2$ cup chopped pecans
$^1/_2$ cup sliced green onions
  1   pound smoked turkey, julienned
      Red and green leaf lettuce

- Whisk sherry into mayonnaise.
- Combine all remaining ingredients except lettuce.
- Serve on crisp leaf lettuce.

Ben Owen (1905-1984)
Jugtown Pottery, c. 1950
Noggin, bowl and creamer
Stoneware with salt glaze and cobalt decoration
Gift of Woodrow W. Pruett and William S. Bridges in memory of Juliana Royster Busbee

In 1921 Juliana and Jacques Busbee founded Jugtown Pottery
in Asheboro, North Carolina. In 1923, Ben Owen
joined this craft center as Jugtown's "Master Potter."

Brunch & Breads

Hobson Pittman (1900-1972)
Roses in Tall Vase, 1965
Oil on canvas
Purchased by the Jessie N. Howell Memorial North Carolina Acquisitions Fund

A native of North Carolina, Hobson Pittman was
a teacher and prodigious painter whose still lifes and
interior scenes are found in museums throughout America.

PULL-APART COFFEE CAKE

YIELD:
Serves 6 - 8

NOTES:
An easy, last-minute coffee cake to impress your family or guests.

3 (10 ounce) cans ready-to-cook biscuits
1 cup butter, melted
1 1/2 cups light brown sugar
2 teaspoons cinnamon
1 cup pecans, chopped

- Grease a Bundt pan.
- Cut biscuits into quarters.
- Add brown sugar, cinnamon and pecans to butter and mix.
- Cover bottom of pan with half of biscuit quarters.
- Pour half of the sugar mixture over biscuits, add second layer, ending with sugar mixture on top.
- Bake at 300° for 40 - 45 minutes. When done, wait 5 minutes, then turn upside down onto a large serving plate.
- To serve, pull apart with fingers.

SAUSAGE AND CHEESE TARTS

YIELD:

Makes 1 dozen

NOTES:

These freeze beautifully. Garnish with cherry tomatoes and parsley.

$^1/_2$ pound pork sausage (or lean ground beef)
1 $^1/_4$ cups biscuit mix
$^1/_4$ cups butter, melted
2 tablespoons boiling water
1 egg, slightly beaten
$^1/_2$ cup half and half
2 tablespoons chopped scallions
$^1/_2$ cup shredded cheddar, Swiss, or mozzarella cheese

- Cook meat in a skillet over medium heat until browned, stirring to crumble. Drain and set aside.

- Combine biscuit mix, butter and boiling water. Stir well.

- Press about 1 tablespoon of dough into bottom and sides of well-greased and floured muffin pans.

- Spoon meat evenly into muffin cups.

- Combine egg, half and half, and scallions in bowl. Stir well.

- Spoon about 2 tablespoons mixture into each cup.

- Bake at 375° for 20 minutes.

- Sprinkle cheese over tarts, and bake an additional 5 minutes.

SWEET POTATO PANCAKES

YIELD:

Makes 8 - 10 pancakes

NOTES:

These are rich and wonderful.

Try them for Sunday brunch.

2 cups self-rising flour
3 tablespoons sugar
$^1/_2$ teaspoon salt
5 tablespoons melted butter
2 whole eggs, lightly beaten
1 $^1/_2$ cups milk
1 cup chopped toasted pecans
$^1/_2$ cup chopped dates
$^1/_2$ cup raisins
2 cups cooked, mashed sweet potatoes
  Vegetable oil
  Maple syrup
  Sour cream

- Sift flour, sugar and salt together.
- Combine remaining ingredients except oil, syrup and sour cream with sweet potatoes in a bowl.
- Stir flour mixture into sweet potato combination. Do not over mix.
- Lightly oil griddle or frying pan and heat.
- Drop batter by spoonfuls and cook until bubbling, then flip over.
- Serve warm with maple syrup and sour cream.

GINGERBREAD PANCAKES

YIELD:

3 ½ cups batter, or 8 - 10 pancakes.

NOTES:

This recipe also makes terrific waffles.

Serve with maple syrup, honey or molasses.

3	eggs
¼	cup brown sugar
½	cup buttermilk
½	cup water (or milk)
¼	cup brewed coffee
2 ½	cups white unbleached flour
½	teaspoon salt
1	teaspoon baking powder
1 ½	teaspoons baking soda
1	teaspoon cloves
1	tablespoon cinnamon
1	tablespoon ginger
1	tablespoon nutmeg
4	tablespoons melted butter

- Cream eggs and brown sugar.

- Stir in buttermilk, water (or milk) and coffee.

- Sift together dry ingredients into a separate bowl.

- Mix egg mixture into flour combination, add butter and stir.

- Cook on a greased heated griddle as you would any other pancake.

NIGHT BEFORE EGGS

YIELD:
Serves 10

NOTES:
Great for morning entertaining.
The French bread makes this dish light and fluffy.

4 cups cubed French bread
2 cups Cheddar cheese, shredded

- Mix and cover the bottom of a 9" x 13" baking dish.

10 eggs
4 cups milk
1 teaspoon dry mustard
1/2 small onion grated

- Mix eggs, milk and seasonings.
- Pour egg mixture over bread and cheese, cover with plastic wrap and refrigerate overnight.

1/2 cup raw red bell pepper
1/2 cup tomatoes
1/2 cup raw mushrooms
10 slices cooked bacon (or 2 cups chopped country ham)
1/4 cup chopped fresh parsley

- Chop above ingredients.
- Bake egg mixture at 350° for 50 minutes.
- Spread vegetable mixture evenly over top of cooked eggs and return to oven for another 10 minutes.

SPINACH QUICHE

Yield:
Serves 6

Notes:
If you're ever caught off-guard, this is a wonderful recipe to have up your sleeve.

1 package frozen spinach soufflé, thawed
2 eggs, well-beaten
  Freshly grated nutmeg
1 cup shredded Swiss cheese
½ cup chopped mushrooms
1 pie crust, uncooked

- Add eggs and nutmeg to spinach soufflé.
- Place cheese and mushrooms in bottom of pie crust.
- Pour spinach on top and bake at 375° for 40 or 45 minutes or until set in center.

LUNCH MUSHROOMS

YIELD:
Serves 4

NOTES:
Serve Lunch Mushrooms with Greek Village Salad (see page 153).

1 red onion, sliced thin
½ red bell pepper, chopped
2 tablespoons olive oil
1 tablespoon sesame oil
1 pound Shiitake (or Portobello) mushrooms, chopped
1 tablespoon cumin
16 ounces sour cream
  Salt and freshly ground pepper to taste
1 French baguette loaf

- Sauté onion and pepper in oils until translucent.
- Add chopped mushrooms and stir 3 - 4 minutes.
- Add cumin and sour cream and stir another 3 - 4 minutes.
- Serve on toasted thick slices of French bread.

HERBED RICOTTA TORTE

YIELD:
Serves 8

NOTES:
Crust is most unusual.
This is also a great
appetizer, served on
crackers.

CRUST:

1 ½ cups stale whole wheat bread crumbs
8 tablespoons butter, softened
1 cup ground almonds

- Combine and press into bottom and sides of a buttered 9" springform pan.

FILLING:

12 ounces cream cheese, cut into bits
1 cup whole milk ricotta
2 large eggs
⅓ cup fresh dill (if unavailable, mix thyme, tarragon and chives)
2 tablespoons half and half
1 teaspoon minced lemon rind
1 teaspoon salt
½ teaspoon nutmeg

- Place all filling ingredients in food processor and process until smooth.
- Pour into crust and bake at 350° for 45 minutes or until a knife inserted into center comes out clean.
- Cool in pan on rack.
- Remove from pan. Garnish with fresh dill or herbs.
- May be prepared one day ahead, covered and refrigerated, then brought to room temperature before serving.

SPANAKOPITA

YIELD:
Serves at least 12

NOTES:
Buttery and flaky, it is a special treat and well worth the effort.

2 pounds fresh spinach
8 large eggs
1 ½ pounds Feta cheese, crumbled
½ pound Cottage cheese
¼ cup chopped fresh dill (or 1 tablespoon dried)
¼ cup olive oil
½ pound unsalted butter, melted
1 pound phyllo pastry sheets, thawed

- Rinse spinach several times. Trim stems, chop leaves and drain.

- Beat eggs in large bowl and stir in cheeses and dill.

- Heat oil in a large skillet and sauté spinach for about 2 minutes, or until wilted.

- Add spinach to cheese mixture, mix well and set aside.

- Preheat oven to 350°. Brush large baking pan (14" x 18") generously with melted butter. (If your pan is smaller, stack phyllo sheets and cut them to fit pan.)

- Place 10 phyllo sheets in pan, one at a time, brushing each one with melted butter. (Keep phyllo covered with a damp dish towel when not in use to prevent drying out.)

- Spread spinach mixture over phyllo layers and top with ten more phyllo sheets, buttering each one.

- With a very sharp knife, cut through top sheet or two to mark serving size pieces.

- Sprinkle with a little water and bake about 50 minutes or until golden brown. Let stand about 20 minutes before cutting along pre-scored lines.

HOT FRUIT CASSEROLE

YIELD:
Serves 12 - 16

NOTES:
If time is a problem, try this sauce instead: Spread 8 ounces sour cream over hot fruit and top with crushed macaroons.

1   lemon
1   orange
3   tablespoons light brown sugar
1   (16 ounce) can apricots, drained
1   (16 ounce) can pineapple chunks, drained
1   (16 ounce) can sliced peaches, drained
1   (16 ounce) can pitted cherries, drained
    Nutmeg, freshly grated
    Honey Dressing (see below)

• Grate rind of the lemon and the orange.

• Combine this zest with brown sugar.

• Slice lemon and orange into rings.

• In a 9" x 13" casserole layer canned fruit with the citrus slices, sprinkling each layer with brown sugar mixture and a dash of nutmeg.

• Bake at 350° for 30 minutes or until hot.

• Top with Honey Dressing and sprinkle with lemon zest and serve.

HONEY DRESSING

YIELD:
About 2 cups

2   eggs
$1/4$ cup fresh lemon juice
2   tablespoons frozen orange juice concentrate
2   tablespoons honey
$1/8$ teaspoon salt
$1/2$ cup whipping cream, whipped
2   tablespoons grated lemon zest for garnish

• In a saucepan, beat eggs.

• Stir in lemon juice, orange juice, honey and salt.

• Cook over low heat until thick, stirring frequently.

• Cool and fold in whipped cream.

MARINER'S OMELET

YIELD:
Serves 2

NOTES:
A delectable Sunday morning treat for two. May be doubled for four.

1 green onion chopped
1 tablespoon red or yellow pepper, chopped
2 large mushrooms, sliced
1 tablespoon butter
6 fresh raw shrimp, shelled and deveined
2 ounces scallops, smoked salmon, or crabmeat
2 tablespoons white wine
2 tablespoons light cream
1 tablespoon butter
4 eggs, beaten until frothy
   Salt and freshly ground pepper
   Sour cream and red caviar for garnish

- Sauté onion, pepper and mushrooms in butter.
- Add shrimp, seafood and white wine.
- Cook until wine has evaporated, then add cream.
- Heat butter in clean skillet or omelet pan, then add eggs and seafood.
- Season with salt and pepper, fold omelet, cook until eggs are no longer runny.
- Top with sour cream and caviar. Serve immediately.

SHRIMP AU GRATIN

YIELD:

Serves 4

NOTES:

Try as an accompaniment to sliced country ham.

1 pound large fresh raw shrimp, peeled
1 tablespoon lemon juice
2 tablespoons butter
3 tablespoons all-purpose flour
$^1/_2$ cup half and half
$^3/_4$ cup white wine
$^1/_2$ teaspoon lemon juice
Salt to taste
$^1/_4$ cup dry bread crumbs
$^1/_4$ cup finely grated Parmesan cheese
Butter

- Preheat oven to 400°.
- Sprinkle shrimp with 1 tablespoon lemon juice.
- Divide shrimp among four ramekins.
- Melt 2 tablespoons butter in small saucepan and stir in flour.
- Gradually add half and half and wine, stirring constantly.
- Cook 5 minutes.
- Season with $^1/_2$ teaspoon lemon juice and salt.
- Spoon sauce over shrimp.
- In a small bowl, combine bread crumbs and cheese. Sprinke over shrimp.
- Dot with butter.
- Bake an additional 12 to 15 minutes, or until topping forms a golden crust.

SHRIMP AND CHEESE SOUFFLÉ

YIELD:

Serves 8

NOTES:

A grand brunch dish because it must be done ahead.

8 pieces white bread, torn into pieces
2 pounds fresh raw shrimp, peeled
2 cups sharp cheddar cheese, grated
¹/₃ cup butter, melted
³/₄ teaspoon dry mustard
    Salt and freshly ground pepper to taste
3 cups milk
¹/₂ cup dry sherry
6 eggs, slightly beaten

- Place bread pieces along bottom of a deep greased casserole.

- Add shrimp and cheese in alternate layers.

- Pour butter over all.

- Add mustard, salt, pepper, milk and sherry to eggs and pour over shrimp and cheese.

- Let stand in refrigerator at least 4 hours or overnight.

- Cover with foil and bake at 350° for one hour.

DEVILED EGGS WITH
SHRIMP AND CRAB MORNAY

YIELD:
Serves 6

NOTES:
Very rich and elegant. Try this exceptional dish to impress the most sophisticated of guests.

10   hard-boiled eggs
$^1/_4$ teaspoon dry mustard
2   tablespoons fresh tarragon (or $^1/_2$ teaspoon dried)
$^3/_4$ cup mayonnaise
1   pound small cooked shrimp (do not overcook)
1   pound backfin crab meat, cleaned (see notes, page 6)
3   scallions, white and green parts, chopped
$^1/_2$ cup freshly grated Parmesan cheese

- Cut eggs in half lengthwise and put yolks in bowl.
- Mash yolks and mix with mustard, tarragon and mayonnaise until smooth.
- Fill each egg white half with yolk mixture.
- Place in a buttered 9" x 13" oven-proof serving dish.
- Arrange shrimp, crab meat and scallions around the eggs.

MORNAY SAUCE:

5   tablespoons butter
5   tablespoons flour
1   (14 $^1/_2$ ounce) can chicken broth
1 $^1/_4$ cups heavy cream
4   ounces Swiss cheese, grated
2   tablespoons dry sherry

- Melt butter and add flour to make a smooth paste, cook while stirring until thick.
- Gradually add chicken broth and cream, stirring constantly.
- Cook, stirring over low heat until sauce is thick and smooth.
- Lower heat and add cheese, stirring until cheese melts.
- Add sherry.

TO ASSEMBLE:

- Spoon sauce over eggs and seafood. Sprinkle with Parmesan cheese.
- Bake at 350° for 15 - 20 minutes until hot and bubbly.
- Broil for 4 minutes to brown top.

FRONT STREET CHIPPED BEEF

YIELD:
Serves 12

NOTES:
Chipped beef has faded from the scene. This version is "Comfort Food" with a new wrinkle.

Try serving it with Hot Fruit Casserole (see page 197).

1   pound chipped beef, cut into 1/2 inch strips
4   tablespoons butter
1   pound mushrooms, sliced
¹/₂ cup minced onion
¹/₂ cup flour
2   cups milk
3   cups light cream
2   (14 ounce) cans artichoke hearts, quartered
3   tablespoons capers, drained
3   tablespoons prepared horseradish
     Salt and freshly ground pepper
1   (14 ounce) can pitted ripe olives
6   English muffins, split

- Soak chipped beef in hot water for 30 minutes and drain.

- Melt 2 tablespoons butter in a large skillet, add beef, onions and mushrooms. Cook until slightly frizzled, about 3 minutes.

- Add remaining butter and flour. Cook, stirring, for 2 minutes.

- Stir in milk and cream. Cook until thickened.

- Blend in artichokes, capers, horseradish, salt and pepper.

- Transfer to a chafing or baking dish, sprinkling the top with olives.

- Keep warm and serve over toasted English muffin halves.

HAM SOUFFLÉ

YIELD:
Serves 24

NOTES:
Great for a crowd and easy to make.

2 ¹/₂   pounds ground ham
2 ¹/₂   pounds grated sharp cheddar
  15   eggs, beaten
2 ¹/₂   quarts milk
  ¹/₂   pound unsalted soda crackers, crumbled
  ¹/₂   teaspoon baking soda
        Hot pepper sauce to taste
   2   cloves garlic, minced, or to taste
        Mushroom Sauce (see below)

- Mix all ingredients. Pour into 2 greased 9" x 13" pans.
- Bake at 350° for 2 hours. Change pans' positions after 1 hour.
- Serve with Mushroom Sauce on the side.

MUSHROOM SAUCE

NOTES:
Try a mixture of Portabella, Shiitake, and Button mushrooms.

   2   pounds assorted mushrooms, sliced
  ¹/₄   pound butter
   2   tablespoons flour
  12   ounces chicken broth
  16   ounces sour cream

- Sauté mushrooms in butter.
- Add flour and stir until smooth.
- Slowly add broth while stirring.
- Lower heat and stir in sour cream.

FRESH MINT TEA

YIELD:
2 quarts

NOTES:
This is a lovely version of the South's traditional drink.

13 tea bags
1/4 cup fresh mint leaves
    Juice of 2 lemons
6 ounces frozen orange juice concentrate
1 cup sugar
    Mint sprigs for garnish

- Combine tea, mint leaves and 1 quart water in large saucepan.
- Cover and bring to a boil. Remove from heat and let steep 30 minutes.
- Add lemon juice, orange juice concentrate, sugar and enough additional water to make 2 quarts.
- Strain and chill. Serve in tall glasses over ice and garnish with mint.

BRUNCH PUNCH

YIELD:
Serves 50

NOTES:
For a festive event add a dry white wine to the punch.

A fruited ice ring can chill the punch.

2 ounces citric acid (available in drug stores)
1 quart boiling water
5 cups sugar
1 (12 ounce) can frozen concentrated orange juice

- Using a wooden spoon, mix citric acid in boiling water until dissolved.
- Stir in sugar and orange juice.
- Divide into two 1 gallon containers.

2 (12 ounce) cans frozen orange juice, mixed as directed
2 (48 ounce) cans pineapple juice

- Add 1 can of each juice to each gallon jug. Chill.

2 (2 litre) bottles of ginger ale

- When ready to serve add 1 bottle of ginger ale to each gallon of punch in punch bowl.

GOOD MORNING MUFFINS

YIELD:

48 medium muffins or 100 miniature muffins

NOTES:

These are great to keep in the freezer, frozen in batches.

Easy to prepare ahead for houseguests or brunch.

4	cups flour
2 1/2	cups sugar
4	teaspoons baking soda
4	teaspoons cinnamon
1	teaspoon salt
1	cup raisins (or chopped dates)
4	cups grated, peeled apples (approximately seven apples)
1	cup chopped pecans
1	cup shredded coconut
1 1/2	cups grated carrots
6	large eggs
1 1/2	cups vegetable oil
4	teaspoons vanilla

- Preheat oven to 350°.

- Grease or paper line 48 muffin cups.

- In a large bowl sift together dry ingredients.

- Stir in fruit, nuts, coconut and carrots and mix until flour is incorporated.

- In another bowl, combine eggs, oil and vanilla. Cream until light and fluffy.

- Add to flour mixture and stir until just blended.

- Spoon batter into muffin cups, filling them 2/3 full.

- Bake for 25 minutes or until muffins are springy to the touch.

- Cool pans 5 minutes on wire rack.

- Remove muffins from pans and cool completely before placing in a closed container.

PECAN ORANGE MUFFINS

YIELD:

*12 regular or
48 miniature muffins*

NOTES:

*"Variety is the spice of
life." A fruited or
sweet bread or muffin
is a nice surprise
added to the bread
basket for breakfast,
lunch, or dinner.*

1   medium size orange, well scrubbed and wiped dry
1/2   cup butter, at room temperature
1   cup plus 1 tablespoon sugar
2   large eggs
1   teaspoon baking soda
2   cups all-purpose flour
1   cup buttermilk
3/4   cup pecans, finely chopped
1/3   cup freshly squeezed orange juice

- Heat oven to 375°.

- Grease muffin cups or use baking cups.

- Finely grate orange peel (no white pith). Juice orange and reserve.

- With an electric mixer beat butter and one cup of sugar until pale and creamy.

- Beat in eggs, one at a time.

- Stir in baking soda and grated peel.

- Fold in half of the flour, then half of the buttermilk.

- Repeat, then fold in pecans.

- Fill prepared muffin cups 3/4 full, and bake 20 to 25 minutes or until browned. Remove from oven.

- Spoon orange juice over hot muffins and sprinkle with 1 tablespoon of sugar.

- Let stand 5 minutes before removing from pan.

IRISH GINGER MUFFINS

YIELD:

36 small muffins or 16 - 20 large

NOTES:

The freshly ground pepper adds a delicious zip!

1 $^1/_2$ cups sifted flour
1 teaspoon baking soda
$^1/_2$ teaspoon ginger
$^1/_2$ teaspoon cinnamon
1 teaspoon freshly ground pepper
$^1/_2$ cup heavy, dark molasses filled up to one cup level with granulated sugar
1 tablespoon butter, melted in 1 cup hot water

- Preheat oven to 450°.
- Put all ingredients in a bowl and stir to mix.
- Batter will be lumpy.
- Pour in greased muffin tins.
- Bake at 450° for 10 - 15 minutes.

ORANGE NUT BREAD

YIELD:

1 loaf

NOTES:

For tea time treats, mix cream cheese with preserved or candied ginger, and spread on this delightful bread.

Or mix cream cheese, marmalade, orange juice and chopped pecans.

3 cups flour
3 teaspoons baking powder
$^1/_2$ teaspoon salt
$^1/_4$ cup sugar
$^1/_2$ cup chopped walnuts (or pecans)
1 tablespoon grated orange peel
$^1/_2$ cup English orange marmalade
1 egg, well-beaten
1 cup milk

- Preheat oven to 350°.
- Sift together all dry ingredients.
- Add remaining ingredients and mix well.
- Pour into well-greased loaf pan and let stand for 10 minutes.
- Bake in 350° oven for about one hour.
- Let cool and slice thin for tea sandwiches, thicker for breakfast toast.

LEMON TEA BREAD

YIELD:
Serves 8

NOTES:
This freezes well.
Try baking in
individual muffin tins.

³/₄ cup sugar
¹/₃ cup butter
1 teaspoon lemon extract
¹/₄ cup fresh lemon juice
2 whole eggs (or 3 egg whites)
1 ¹/₂ cups plain flour
1 teaspoon baking powder
¹/₂ cup skim milk
  Grated rind of 1 lemon
³/₄ cup slivered almonds
¹/₃ cup brown sugar
1 teaspoon flour

- Preheat oven to 350°.
- With an electric hand mixer, cream sugar and butter.
- Add lemon extract and lemon juice. Blend and beat in eggs, one at a time.
- Sift flour with baking powder and stir in alternately with milk.
- Add lemon rind and ¹/₂ cup almonds.
- Pour into greased bread pan; top with mixture of brown sugar, ¹/₄ cup almonds and flour.
- Bake at 350° for 30 minutes or until toothpick inserted in center comes out clean.
- Remove from oven and make several holes in top with a skewer. Pour topping over loaf.
- Cool in pan. Remove and store in refrigerator.

TOPPING:
¹/₂ cup powdered sugar
¹/₄ cup lemon juice

- Combine topping ingredients.

HARVEST ZUCCHINI BREAD

YIELD:
2 loaves

NOTES:
This is a tangy bread served at any meal.

3 eggs
3 cups brown sugar
2 cups grated zucchini
3 cups unsifted flour
1 teaspoon salt
1 teaspoon nutmeg
1 teaspoon black pepper
1 teaspoon baking soda
1 cup coconut
1 cup walnuts (or pecans), chopped
1 cup raisins (or chopped dried fruit)
1 teaspoon ground allspice
1 teaspoon cinnamon
1 cup oil
1 tablespoon vanilla

- Preheat oven to 325°.

- Mix all ingredients thoroughly.

- Pour into 2 large loaf pans. Bake at 325° for 1 hour and 10 minutes.

SAUSAGE BREAKFAST BREAD

YIELD:
Serves 12

NOTES:

This is a sensational sweet breakfast bread.

The bread can be stored, wrapped in plastic wrap and foil in the refrigerator.

It makes a welcome Christmas or hostess gift.

1	cup raisins
1	pound pork sausage
1 ½	cups brown sugar
1 ½	cups sugar
2	eggs, beaten
3	cups flour
1	teaspoon ginger
1	teaspoon baking powder
1	teaspoon pumpkin pie spice
1	teaspoon baking soda
1	cup cold strong coffee
1	cup chopped pecans (or walnuts)

- Preheat oven to 350°.
- Simmer raisins in a little water for 4 - 5 minutes. Drain and set aside.
- Mix sausage and sugars until well blended.
- Add eggs and mix well.
- Sift flour, ginger, baking powder and spices.
- Stir soda into coffee.
- Add flour mixture and coffee alternately to meat mixture, beating well after each addition.
- Stir in raisins and nuts, and pour into greased and floured 9-inch tube pan.
- Bake at 350° for 1 ½ hours until toothpick comes out clean.

PAPRIKA TOAST

YIELD:

24 toast points

NOTES:

These are crisp and wonderful to serve warm with a salad luncheon.

12 slices white bread, thinly sliced
$1/4$ cup sweet butter, melted
$1/4$ teaspoon salt
$1/4$ teaspoon pepper
1 $1/2$ teaspoons sweet paprika

- Preheat oven to 375°.
- Cut crusts off bread, and slice in half diagonally.
- Mix butter, salt, pepper and paprika.
- Brush butter mixture on both sides of bread.
- Place on cookie sheet and bake 20 minutes at 375°, turning once to brown evenly.

BUTTERMILK BISCUITS

YIELD:

Makes 5 dozen 1" biscuits

NOTES:

Freezes well after baking.

The secret to biscuits is not to overwork dough.

1 package yeast
2 tablespoons warm water (105°-115°)
5 cups self-rising flour
1 cup vegetable shortening
2 cups buttermilk

- Preheat oven to 400°.
- Add yeast to warm water to proof (as per package directions).
- Place flour in bowl and cut in shortening.
- Stir yeast into buttermilk.
- Add buttermilk to flour mixture and blend to form dough.
- Roll out on floured board to a uniform $1/2$-inch thickness and cut to desired size.
- Place on ungreased cookie sheet. Bake at 400° for 15 to 20 minutes until brown.

CREAM CHEESE ROPES

YIELD:

Serves 8 for each braid - 32 in all

NOTES:

Rope dough must be made a day ahead.

This will freeze, but warm in oven before serving.

ROPE DOUGH:

1	cup sour cream
$^1/_2$	cup sugar
1	teaspoon salt
$^1/_2$	cup butter, melted
$^1/_2$	cup warm water (105° -115°)
2	packages dry yeast
2	eggs, beaten
2	cups all-purpose flour

- Heat sour cream over low heat, stirring in sugar, salt and butter. Cool to lukewarm.

- Pour warm water into a large mixing bowl, sprinkle yeast over water. Stir until yeast dissolves. Let sit 5 minutes.

- Add sour cream mixture, eggs and flour.

- Mix well, cover tightly with plastic wrap and refrigerate overnight.

CREAM CHEESE FILLING:

2	(8 ounce) packages cream cheese, softened
$^3/_4$	cup sugar
1	egg beaten
	Pinch of salt
2	teaspoons vanilla

- Combine all ingredients and mix well.

TO ASSEMBLE:

- Divide dough into four equal parts, and roll each part out on a floured board into a 12" by 8" rectangle.
- Spread one-fourth cream cheese filling on each rectangle, and roll up, jelly-roll fashion, beginning at the long sides.
- Pinch edges together and fold ends under slightly.
- Place rolls seam side down on greased baking sheets.
- Slit each roll at 2-inch intervals diagonally about two-thirds of the way through dough.
- Cover and let rise in a warm place, free from drafts, until doubled in bulk (about one hour).
- Bake at 375° for 15 - 20 minutes. Spread with glaze while warm.

GLAZE:

2   cups powdered sugar
4   tablespoons milk
2   teaspoons vanilla

- Combine all ingredients in a small bowl and mix well.

HERB SWIRL ROLLS

YIELD:
Serves 8

NOTES:

Use fresh herbs whenever possible. If you must use dry, the ratio is three fresh to one dry.

To enhance this filling, add shredded prosciutto.

1 (16 ounce) package of frozen bread dough
3 tablespoons butter, melted
2 tablespoons chives, chopped
2 tablespoons parsley, minced
1 tablespoon dill or basil or thyme
$^{1}/_{4}$ teaspoon garlic powder
   Freshly ground pepper
$^{1}/_{4}$ cup freshly grated Parmesan cheese
1 egg
2 tablespoons poppy seeds

- Thaw frozen dough according to package directions.

- On a lightly floured board, roll dough into about a 9" by 12" rectangle.

- Spread melted butter over dough.

- Mix herbs, pepper and cheese over butter.

- Beginning with long side of rectangle, roll dough tightly as in a jelly roll.

- Cut dough roll into 12 equal pieces and place on a lightly greased cookie sheet.

- Mix egg with 2 tablespoons water and brush on each roll. Sprinkle with poppy seeds.

- Let rise 30 minutes.

- Bake at 375° for 12 - 15 minutes or until golden brown.

THREE CHEESE BREAD

YIELD:
Serves 10

NOTES:
Great companion for hot soups such as Oyster & Corn Chowder (see page 36) or Souper Spinach (see page 32).

$^1/_4$ pound natural Swiss cheese
$^1/_4$ pound sharp Cheddar cheese
4 $^1/_2$ cups all-purpose flour
2 teaspoons sugar
$^1/_4$ teaspoon salt
2 packages yeast
1 cup warm water (105° - 115°)
1 cup butter
6 eggs, beaten
$^1/_2$ cup freshly grated Parmesan cheese

- Cut Swiss and Cheddar cheeses into $^1/_4$-inch cubes, and set aside.

- Combine flour, sugar and salt.

- Proof yeast in warm water (as per package directions).

- With an electric mixer, cream butter. Mix in eggs and yeast.

- Gradually add flour and beat until very smooth.

- Stir in cheese cubes and Parmesan. Cover and let rise until double in bulk.

- Grease a large tube pan. Stir down dough, put in pan, cover and let rise again until doubled in size.

- Bake at 350° for about 40 minutes. Let cool 20 minutes before removing from pan.

TOMATO BASIL BREAD

YIELD:
2 loaves

NOTES:
This is even good toasted for breakfast.

How about a grilled Portobello mushroom sandwich with this bread?

1/3 cup olive oil
1 onion, chopped
1 cup oil-packed sun-dried tomatoes, chopped
1/2 cup fresh basil (or 2 tablespoons dried)
4 1/2 cups flour
1 tablespoon sugar
1 tablespoon salt
2 packages yeast
1 1/2 cups warm water (105°-115°)

- Sauté onion, tomato, and basil in olive oil. Cool.

- Combine 3 cups flour with sugar, salt and yeast. Add warm water, and stir.

- Add sautéed ingredients and remaining flour. Knead for 10 minutes.

- Cover and let rise in warm place 1 hour or until doubled in size.

- Put into 2 greased loaf pans and let rise until doubled again.

- Bake at 400° for 35 minutes or until done.

BACON CORNBREAD

YIELD:

8 servings

NOTES:

For added color, add 3 1/2 ounce can chopped green chilies, and 1 small red pepper, seeded and diced, with the corn and bacon.

6   slices bacon
1   cup flour
1   cup yellow cornmeal
1/2 teaspoon salt
1   teaspoon sugar
2   teaspoons baking powder
2   eggs, beaten
1   cup milk
1   cup corn kernels, canned, drained, or frozen, thawed

- Preheat oven to 425°.

- Cut bacon into 1/4-inch strips and place in an ovenproof skillet.

- Cook over high heat until very brown and crisp. Remove and drain.

- Combine dry ingredients in a bowl and mix.

- Add eggs and half the milk. Mix until smooth.

- Stir in the remaining milk, corn and bacon.

- Pour mixture back into the skillet on top of the bacon grease.

- Place in a 425° oven for 20 minutes.

ZUCCHINI BREAD

YIELD:
2 loaves

NOTES:
A secret recipe well worth trying.

3   eggs
2   cups sugar
1   cup oil
2   teaspoons vanilla
2   cups shredded zucchini
1   (7 ounce) can crushed pineapple
1   cup chopped nuts
3   cups flour
2   teaspoons baking soda
1   teaspoon salt
$^1/_2$ teaspoon baking powder
1 $^1/_2$ teaspoons cinnamon
$^3/_4$ teaspoon nutmeg

- Preheat oven to 350°.
- Beat eggs until foamy.
- Beat in sugar, oil and vanilla until thick and foamy.
- Stir in zucchini and pineapple.
- Sift together dry ingredients and add nuts.
- Fold in zucchini mixture.
- Pour into 2 loaf pans.
- Bake at 350° for 50 - 60 minutes.

Desserts

Elisabeth A. Chant (1865-1947)
Minnesota Studio, c. 1900
Oil on canvas
Gift of Henry J. MacMillan

Born in England, Elisabeth Chant immigrated to Minnesota with her family at the age of 13. In 1901 she returned to England for two years. This experience acquainted her with the Arts and Crafts movement and a style of painting referred to a Rustic Naturalism. From 1922, Chant resided in Wilmington, North Carolina, where she painted, taught art classes and founded the Wilmington Museum of Art which was in existence from 1938 to 1941.

PECAN LACE COOKIES

YIELD:

90 - 100 cookies

NOTES:

These are so good they have to be hidden!

Sometime, try melting semi-sweet chocolate, dipping tines of fork into chocolate and dribbling it over cooled cookies.

Make these only on a dry day.

1   cup pecan pieces
1   cup sugar
1/4 cup flour
1/4 teaspoon baking powder
1/4 teaspoon salt
8   tablespoons butter, melted
1   teaspoon vanilla
1   egg
     Pecan halves

- Preheat oven to 325°.

- Grind pecan pieces and sugar in food processor.

- Add rest of dry ingredients and mix, then add butter, vanilla and egg.

- Line cookie sheets with foil. Do not grease the foil.

- Drop *tiny* amounts on pans, pressing a pecan half on each one to flatten. These really spread out while cooking.

- Bake for 8 minutes at 325°. Place foil on rack, and let cookies cool completely (10 minutes) before peeling off foil.

ORANGE CHOCOLATE CHIP COOKIES

YIELD:

4 dozen

NOTES:

The orange zest makes this variation on a classic exciting.

1 cup unsalted butter, softened
²/₃ cup packed light brown sugar
²/₃ cup sugar
1 large egg
1 teaspoon vanilla
1 ³/₄ cups all-purpose flour
½ teaspoon baking soda
¼ teaspoon salt
6 ounces best quality bittersweet chocolate, broken into pieces
3 ounces good-quality milk chocolate broken into pieces
1 ½ cups old-fashioned rolled oats
1 cup sweetened grated coconut
1 cup pecans, coarsely chopped
Zest of three oranges, minced

- Preheat oven to 375°.

- In a large bowl, cream butter, brown sugar and sugar with an electric mixer until fluffy.

- Beat in the egg and vanilla.

- With a wooden spoon, stir in flour, baking soda and salt.

- Fold in chocolate, oats, coconut, pecans and zest.

- Drop a rounded tablespoon about 2 inches apart on lightly greased cookie sheet.

- Bake about 12 minutes, or until golden brown. Transfer to rack to cool.

FRENCH SILK TARTS

YIELD:
30 miniature tarts

NOTES:
These are for chocolate lovers!

1/2	cup plus 2 tablespoons butter, softened
1	cup sugar
2	squares unsweetened chocolate, melted and cooled
1	tablespoon unsweetened cocoa
1 1/2	teaspoons vanilla
2	drops almond extract
3	eggs
	Purchased miniature tart shells
	Confectioners' sugar

- Combine butter and sugar until light, using electric mixer.
- Stir in chocolate, cocoa, and flavors.
- Add eggs, one at a time, beating thoroughly after each addition.
- Chill mixture 1 - 2 hours.
- Just before serving, spoon into miniature tart shells.
- Dust tops with confectioners' sugar.

SAND TART COOKIES

YIELD:

*2 - 3 dozen
4-inch cookies*

NOTES:

*Dough must be
prepared 24 hours
in advance.*

*A wonderful old
Southern family
recipe.*

COOKIE DOUGH:

$^1/_2$	cup butter, softened
1	cup sugar
1	egg, well beaten
1 $^3/_4$	cups all purpose flour
2	teaspoons baking powder

- Cream butter until fluffy. Add sugar slowly and continue beating. Add egg.

- Sift together flour and baking powder. Add slowly to butter mixture.

- Pat into a ball, cover with plastic wrap and refrigerate 24 hours.

- Roll $^1/_8$ inch thick on lightly floured surface. Cut shapes from dough with cookie cutter.

- Place two inches apart on lightly greased pan.

TO DECORATE AND BAKE:

1	egg white, beaten with 1 teaspoon water
1	tablespoon white sugar
$^1/_4$	teaspoon cinnamon
$^1/_2$	cup thinly sliced blanched almonds

- Brush cookie tops with egg white wash.

- Sprinkle sugar mixed with cinnamon on tops.

- Decoratively place the almond slivers on top of each cookie.

- Bake for 8 minutes at 325°. Cookies should be golden but not brown.

- Remove from pan onto waxed paper to cool. Store in air tight container.

OATMEAL MACAROONS

YIELD:

4 dozen
3-inch cookies

NOTES:

Moist and delicious!

For a quicker version,
bake for 35 minutes
in a 9" x 13" pan,
and cut into squares.

1 cup butter, softened
1 cup sugar
1 cup brown sugar
2 eggs
1 teaspoon vanilla
1 teaspoon baking powder
1 teaspoon soda
2 cups flour
1 cup oatmeal
1 cup moist coconut
1 cup chopped pecans (or walnuts)

- Preheat oven to 350°.

- Cream together butter, sugar and brown sugar.

- Add eggs and vanilla and beat well.

- Mix baking powder and baking soda with flour, add to creamed mixture. Stir in oatmeal, coconut, and nuts.

- Drop by spoonfuls onto lightly greased cookie sheet.

- Bake at 350° for 12 minutes, or until delicately browned.

CHEESECAKE BROWNIES

YIELD:

Makes 24 bars

NOTES:

This is a rich, chewy brownie.

It's just right for a finger-food dessert.

For a plated dessert serve à la mode. Don't forget the hot fudge and nuts!

$^1/_2$ cup butter

8 ounces cream cheese, softened

1 $^1/_2$ cups sugar

3 eggs

1 teaspoon instant coffee granules, dissolved in 1 $^1/_2$ teaspoons hot water

$^3/_4$ cup all-purpose flour

$^1/_2$ cup unsweetened cocoa

$^1/_2$ teaspoon baking powder

$^1/_2$ teaspoon salt

1 $^1/_2$ teaspoons vanilla extract

1 $^1/_2$ cups semi-sweet chocolate chips

$^3/_4$ cup chopped pecans (or walnuts)

- Preheat oven to 350°.
- Cream butter, cream cheese and sugar until light and fluffy.
- Add eggs, one at a time, beating well after each addition.
- Stir coffee solution into butter and egg mixture.
- Mix flour, cocoa, baking powder and salt.
- Add to cream cheese mixture and stir well.
- Add vanilla, chocolate chips and nuts, stirring to mix thoroughly.
- Pour batter into greased 9" x 13" pan, and bake at 350° for 25 minutes. Cool and cut into squares.

"HEATH" BARS

YIELD:
24 squares

NOTES:
Yummy and sinfully rich.

2 cups flour
1 cup brown sugar
1/2 cup butter, softened
1 cup pecan halves
1 cup butter
3/4 cup brown sugar
12 ounces milk chocolate chips

- Preheat oven to 350°.
- Mix flour, brown sugar and softened butter in food processor or by hand until crumbly.
- Pat lightly into a 9" x 13" ungreased pan.
- Place pecan halves on top of crust.
- Mix butter and brown sugar in saucepan and heat until it boils, stirring constantly. Dribble over pecans.
- Bake at 350° for 18 - 22 minutes.
- Immediately sprinkle with chocolate chips, and spread with spatula when softened.
- Refrigerate until chocolate sets. Cut into squares.

VERY BRITISH TOFFEE

YIELD:

About 3 dozen pieces

NOTES:

These freeze beautifully, and make wonderful gifts.

Don't attempt this recipe on a hot, humid day.

1   cup sugar
1   cup butter
3   tablespoons water
1   teaspoon vanilla extract
1   cup chocolate chips (or 8 ounces semi-sweet chocolate)
³/₄ cup finely chopped pecans (or almonds)

- Line a cookie sheet with foil and butter well.
- Combine sugar, butter and water in a heavy 3-quart saucepan.
- Cook on high heat, stirring occasionally until it reaches a hard crack stage (300° on a candy thermometer, or when a drop of candy turns brittle when dropped in a glass of water). The color will be dark brown.
- Add vanilla, stir and pour mixture onto buttered cookie sheet. It will cover the entire pan.
- Place chocolate chips on top while still hot and spread evenly until chocolate has melted.
- Sprinkle nuts over top.
- Cool thoroughly and break into pieces.

APRICOT MOUSSE

YIELD:
Serves 6

NOTES:
A lovely pastel dessert as pleasing to the eye as to the palate.

1   (6 ounce) box dried apricots
1   cup sugar
2   tablespoons Grand Marnier
1   cup heavy cream, whipped
12   lady fingers, split in half

- In a small saucepan, place apricots and water to cover. Simmer until soft and strain.

- Leave 12 apricots in strainer to dry for use as garnish.

- Mash remaining apricots, adding sugar and Grand Marnier.

- Blend in a little of the whipped cream, then fold in remaining cream.

- Line sides of six large wine glasses with lady finger halves. Place one whole apricot on bottom of glass.

- Fill glasses with apricot-whipped cream mixture and top with a reserved apricot. Chill several hours.

CRÈME FRAMBOISE

YIELD:
Serves 12

NOTES:
This can be made ahead.

It's elegant, easy and very rich.

1   package unflavored gelatin
³/₄ cup sugar
2   cups heavy cream
1   tablespoon vanilla
2   cups sour cream
1   tablespoon brandy
1   (12 ounce) package frozen raspberries, thawed and puréed in blender

- Put gelatin, sugar and heavy cream in a saucepan and let stand 5 minutes.

- Heat over low heat, stirring, until gelatin dissolves. Let cool to lukewarm.

- Add vanilla and sour cream and mix well.

- Mix brandy into raspberry purée and place 1 teaspoonful into bottom of clear, stemmed wine goblets.

- Fill goblets with cream mixture and chill at least 2 hours.

- Serve remaining raspberry sauce separately.

HONEY AND WHISKY CREAM

YIELD:

Serves 8

NOTES:

This is a rich Scottish Highlands version of a flan.

Dietetic it is not, but soothing on a chilly evening.

1 cup heavy cream
4 tablespoons Scotch whisky
4 tablespoons thick honey
4 egg yolks

- Whip the cream, gradually adding whisky, until fairly thick.

- Warm the honey in a saucepan until hot and runny.

- Put the yolks into a bowl. Using an electric mixer, whisk the yolks, gradually pouring in the hot honey.

- Beat until the mixture is thin and pale. This and the cream-whisky should have about the same consistency.

- Fold both mixtures together and divide between 8 individual serving dishes.

- Freeze, and when firm on the surface, cover with a piece of plastic wrap.

- After 3 or 4 hours, serve, garnished with a strawberry or raspberry.

ORANGE SOUFFLÉ

YIELD:
Serves 8

NOTES:
*Perfect for a luncheon
or a bridal shower.*

3 eggs, separated
$^1/_2$ cup sugar
  Grated rind of 3 oranges
1 cup orange juice
1 envelope gelatin
2 cups heavy cream
  Orange sections for garnish

- Beat egg yolks and $^1/_2$ cup sugar about five minutes until light.
- Stir in grated orange rind and $^3/_4$ cup orange juice.
- Soften gelatin in $^1/_4$ cup cold orange juice.
- Heat slowly until gelatin is dissolved.
- Beat gelatin mixture into egg-orange mixture.
- Whip 3 egg whites until very stiff.
- In a separate bowl, whip 2 cups heavy cream.
- Fold egg whites and 1 $^1/_3$ cups whipped cream into egg-orange mixture.
- Pour into individual stemmed goblets, or hollowed-out orange shells, and chill thoroughly.
- Garnish with orange sections and remaining whipped cream.

CHOCOLATE LEAVES

YIELD:
3 dozen

NOTES:
A supremely elegant way to decorate a special dessert.

Mint leaves may be dipped in chocolate, chilled and frozen to add a chocolate-mint flavor.

6 ounces bittersweet chocolate
2 teaspoons solid white shortening
   Leaves: Camellia, citrus, ivy, rose, mint or other decorative non-poisonous leaves (check with your local florist)

- Wipe leaves clean and dry carefully with paper towels.
- Using a double boiler, heat water to a simmer.
- Melt chocolate and shortening and stir. *Do not allow water and chocolate to mix.*
- Using a pastry brush or a spoon, coat the underside (non-shiny) of a leaf with the chocolate.
- Transfer leaf chocolate side up to a cold baking sheet covered with wax paper.
- Chill 30 minutes. Peel away the leaf from the chocolate. You may want to use tweezers so the heat from your hands doesn't melt the chocolate.
- Refrigerate or freeze leaves in an air-tight container, with wax paper between layers.

RASPBERRY SAUCE

YIELD:
Serves 8

NOTES:
Quick and easy.

Great over lemon sorbet, pound cake or orange soufflé.

1 (10 ounce) package frozen raspberries, thawed
   Sugar to taste
1 tablespoon framboise (raspberry liqueur)

- Purée raspberries and strain to eliminate the seeds.
- Put the puree in a pot, add sugar. Bring to a simmer and cook, stirring until sugar dissolves.
- Add framboise and cool sauce completely before serving.

FROZEN CHOCOLATE MOUSSE CAKE

YIELD:
Serves 12

NOTES:
This cake must be frozen for at least 5 hours before serving.

Try strawberries dipped in chocolate for a lovely garnish.

This cake may be frozen up to a week before serving.

GENOISE CAKE CRUST:

1	cup unsalted butter
4	ounces unsweetened chocolate
2	cups sugar
3	large eggs
1	teaspoon vanilla extract
1/2	teaspoon salt
1	cup flour

- Preheat oven to 350°.

- Melt 1/2 of the butter with the chocolate and set aside.

- Cream remaining butter with sugar until light.

- Add eggs, vanilla and salt, and stir in chocolate mixture.

- Gradually fold in flour. Spread batter over 1/2 to 3/4 of a greased and floured jelly roll pan.

- Bake at 350° for 20 -25 minutes, or until a toothpick inserted in center comes out clean. Crust should be soft and chewy.

- When cool, cut to fit bottom of a 10" springform pan. Take a small cookie cutter to make decorative designs from the remaining crust.

MOUSSE:

2	eggs, separated
1	whole egg
3/4	cup sugar
12	ounces dark semi-sweet chocolate, melted
2	teaspoons vanilla extract
3	tablespoons coffee liqueur
1 1/2	tablespoons instant coffee granules
1	cup heavy cream, whipped

- Beat yolks and whole egg until very thick and lemon colored.

- Slowly add 1/2 cup sugar, and beat until thick.

- Add the liquid melted chocolate, vanilla, coffee liqueur and instant coffee granules. Mix well and set aside.

- In another bowl, beat egg whites with clean beaters until foamy.

- Slowly add 1/4 cup sugar and continue beating until stiff but not dry.

- Fold egg whites into chocolate mixture, then fold in whipped cream. Spoon onto crust, and freeze 5 hours or overnight.

- Unmold 15 minutes before serving, and decorate with additional whipped cream and crust cut-outs.

LEMON MOUSSE

YIELD:
Serves 10

NOTES:
This is superb, and can be frozen for 2 weeks.

Decorate with Chocolate Leaves (see page 233) or lemon slices.

CRUST:

1 ³/₄ cups crushed vanilla wafers
5 tablespoons melted butter

- Preheat oven to 375°.

- Mix wafers and butter and press into a greased 10" springform pan.

- Bake at 375° for 5 to 8 minutes until golden. Cool completely.

MOUSSE:

4 egg yolks
¹/₂ cup fresh lemon juice, strained
1 cup sugar
Rind from 1 ¹/₂ lemons, grated
4 egg whites
¹/₈ teaspoon cream of tartar
¹/₈ teaspoon salt
2 cups whipping cream
Enough whole wafers to place on sides of pan

- Combine egg yolks, lemon juice, ¹/₄ cup sugar and rind; beat until thick. Set aside at room temperature.

- Beat egg whites until foamy. Add cream of tartar and salt. Continue beating while adding ³/₄ cup sugar slowly until whites are thick and glossy.

- In separate bowl, beat cream until stiff.

- Fold cream into egg whites, then fold into yolk and lemon mixture.

- Pour half of the mixture over crust, then push whole wafers along sides so they are upright.

- Pour remaining mixture carefully over top. Cover with foil and freeze at least 8 hours. Let soften in refrigerator for one hour before serving.

POACHED PEARS WITH GRAND MARNIER SAUCE

YIELD:
Serves 4

NOTES:
Well worth the trouble!
This is a great finale to a special dinner.

4   ripe pears
2   cups water
1   cup sugar

- Peel pears, leaving stems on. Core pears from blossom ends.
- Bring 2 cups water and 1 cup sugar to boil.
- Carefully add pears, stem side up, and reduce heat. Cover and simmer for 20 minutes, or until pears are tender.
- Remove from heat and let pears cool in liquid.
- Make sauce while pears are poaching.

GRAND MARNIER SAUCE:

2   egg yolks, beaten
2   tablespoons water
$1/4$ cup sugar
2   tablespoons Grand Marnier
$1/2$ cup heavy cream

- Place egg yolks, 2 tablespoons water and $1/4$ cup sugar in top of double boiler over simmering water.
- Beat with electric hand mixer on medium speed for 8 - 10 minutes until very thick, light and pale yellow.
- Remove from heat and transfer to small bowl. Immediately stir in Grand Marnier. Cool for 10 minutes.
- Meanwhile, wash beaters and in another clean bowl, beat cream until stiff peaks form. Fold whipped cream into egg mixture.

TO SERVE:

- Remove pears from liquid and drain well.
- Spoon Grand Marnier sauce onto dessert plates, and place pear on top of sauce. Spoon remaining sauce over pears.
- Garnish with mint or strawberries.

SLICED ORANGES IN SYRUP

YIELD:
Serves 8

NOTES:

Make at least one day ahead for best flavor.

For a richer dessert serve with Sand Tart Cookies (see page 224), Oatmeal Macaroons (see page 225) or Yogurt Cake (see page 246).

8 navel oranges
1 cup water
1/2 cup sugar
3 tablespoons Grand Marnier
   Fresh mint for garnish

- Peel oranges, reserving the peel, and remove pith with a paring knife.

- Slice oranges into rounds and put in glass bowl.

- Cut peel in very thin strips. Place in non-metal saucepan with water to cover and boil for 5 minutes. Drain and remove peel.

- Put sugar and 1 cup water in saucepan and boil for 5 minutes.

- Remove from heat. Stir in orange peel and Grand Marnier. Allow to cool and pour over oranges.

- Chill until ready to serve.

- Garnish with fresh mint.

GRAPES GERVAISE

YIELD:
Serves 4

NOTES:

Effortless and delectable.

If grapes are large, cut them in half.

1 pound seedless grapes, washed, with stems removed
16 ounces sour cream
1/2 cup brown sugar
4 ounces brandy or crème de cacao

- Arrange grapes in wine glasses or in a crystal bowl.

- Mix sour cream, brown sugar, and brandy. Spoon over the grapes just before serving.

ORTON PLANTATION ORANGE PIE

YIELD:

Serves 6

NOTES:

An old family's recipe with wonderful orange flavor.

Try making in individual tart shells, cutting down baking time to 20 - 25 minutes, or until set.

A 9" pie shell
3 eggs, beaten
1 cup sugar
  Juice and grated rind of 2 large oranges
2 tablespoons butter, softened
1 tablespoon corn meal

- Bake pie shell at 350° for ten minutes.

- Cream sugar and butter together.

- Add eggs, orange juice, rind and corn meal. Mix thoroughly.

- Pour into pie shell.

- Bake at 325° for 30 to 40 minutes or until set. Cool before serving.

BLUEBERRY TORTE

YIELD:

Serves 6 - 8

NOTES:

This dessert must be chilled for four hours before serving.

The uncooked berries make this interesting.

A patriotic dessert for the Fourth of July garnished with strawberries.

DOUGH CRUST:

1/3	cup butter
1/4	cup sugar
1	egg yolk
1	teaspoon finely grated orange peel
1	tablespoon fresh orange juice
1/2	teaspoon vanilla
1 1/4	cups all-purpose flour

- Preheat oven to 350°.
- With an electric mixer, combine butter and sugar, beating until fluffy. Add egg yolk, orange peel, juice and vanilla and mix well.
- Gradually add flour, beating at low speed until combined.
- Press into bottom and an inch up the sides of a 10" springform pan. Prick crust with fork.
- Bake at 350° about 20 minutes or until lightly browned.

FILLING:

4 cups fresh blueberries, washed and stems removed
2 tablespoons cornstarch
2 tablespoons water
$1/2$ cup light corn syrup
2 teaspoons lemon juice
1 cup whipping cream
2 tablespoons powdered sugar

- Purée 1 cup blueberries in blender or processor and set aside.

- Combine cornstarch and water in medium saucepan, stirring until blended.

- Add corn syrup, lemon juice and blueberry purée. Bring to a boil, stirring constantly.

- Boil one minute. Cool one hour.

- Fold remaining 3 cups blueberries into mixture. Set aside.

- Beat whipping cream until foamy. Gradually add powdered sugar, and beat until soft peaks form.

TO ASSEMBLE:

- Spread whipped cream in bottom and up sides of crust, forming a 1-inch edge all around.

- Spoon berry mixture over whipped cream shell. Do not mix. Chill at least 4 hours.

COFFEE-TOFFEE PIE

YIELD:
Serves 8

NOTES:
Best if made a day ahead because coffee flavor intensifies overnight.
Sinfully rich and fabulous.

CRUST:

3/4 cup dry pie crust mix
1/4 cup light brown sugar
1 teaspoon vanilla
1 tablespoon water
1 square unsweetened chocolate, grated
3/4 cup walnuts, finely chopped

- Combine above ingredients and place in a 9" pie pan. Spread up sides and across bottom, but do not pat firmly.
- Bake at 375° for 15 minutes. Cool.

FILLING:

1/2 cup butter, softened
3/4 cup white sugar
2 teaspoons instant coffee granules
2 eggs
1 square unsweetened chocolate, melted and cooled

- Beat butter until creamy and add sugar, beating until light.
- Blend in coffee granules and eggs, one at a time, beating 5 minutes after each one. Stir in cooled chocolate. Filling should be thick and creamy.
- Pour filling into pie shell and refrigerate, covered, 2 hours or overnight.

TOPPING:

2 cups heavy cream
2 tablespoons instant coffee granules
1/2 cup confectioners' sugar
Chocolate curls or Chocolate Leaves for decoration

- Two or more hours before serving, mix all topping ingredients and refrigerate, covered, for one hour. Beat until stiff and spread over pie. Decorate top with chocolate curls or Chocolate Leaves (see page 233) and serve.

BOURBON PUMPKIN PIE

YIELD:

Serves 12

NOTES:

*A variation on the
Thanksgiving classic.*

*Can be topped with
whipped cream or
vanilla ice cream and
sprinkled with freshly
grated nutmeg.*

2	cups pumpkin purée, canned or fresh
$^3/_4$	cup packed brown sugar
3	eggs, beaten
$^1/_2$	cup heavy cream
$^1/_2$	cup milk
$^1/_4$	cup Bourbon
1	teaspoon ground cinnamon
$^1/_4$	teaspoon ground cloves
$^1/_2$	teaspoon ground ginger
	Pinch of nutmeg
	Pinch of salt
2	unbaked 9" pie shells
$^3/_4$	cup crushed walnuts
2	tablespoons butter, melted
$^1/_4$	cup packed light brown sugar

- Preheat oven to 400°.

- In a mixing bowl whisk all ingredients listed above pie shell together.

- Pour into pie shells and bake at 400° for 10 minutes.

- Mix walnuts, butter and brown sugar and sprinkle on top of each pie.

- Reduce heat to 350° and bake for 45 minutes or until set.

FRESH PEAR CAKE

YIELD:

Serves 16

NOTES:

Light and perfect after a heavy meal.

If a cake sticks to the pan, cover the bottom of the pan with a wet cloth for a few minutes.

4   cups fresh pears, grated (about 5 pears, peeled and seeded)
    Do not use Bosc pears
2   cups sugar
1   cup pecans, chopped
1   cup vegetable oil
1   teaspoon vanilla extract
2   eggs, beaten
3   cups all-purpose flour
$^1/_2$ teaspoon salt
2   teaspoons baking soda
1   teaspoon freshly grated nutmeg

- Preheat oven to 350°.

- In a large bowl, combine pears, sugar and pecans. Set aside for 1 hour to allow juice to accumulate.

- Using a wooden spoon, stir oil, vanilla and eggs into pear mixture.

- Add remaining dry ingredients and blend until smooth.

- Pour batter into a buttered and floured large tube pan.

- Bake for one hour and 15 minutes, or until toothpick inserted comes out clean. *Do not overcook.* Cake should be moist.

HARVEST APPLE CAKE

YIELD:
Serves 12

NOTES:
A very moist apple spice cake.

Can be served at Christmas instead of fruit cake.

1 ½ cups cooking oil
2 cups sugar
4 beaten eggs
3 cups all-purpose flour
1 teaspoon baking soda
1 teaspoon salt
1 teaspoon allspice
2 teaspoons vanilla extract
3 cups peeled and diced tart apples
1 cup pecans (or walnuts), chopped
1 cup golden raisins

- Mix oil, sugar and eggs together until light.
- Sift flour, baking soda, salt and allspice. Add slowly to egg mixture and stir well.
- Add vanilla, apples, nuts and raisins to batter and mix well.
- Pour into greased and floured tube (angel food) pan.
- Bake at 350° for 60 minutes or until toothpick comes out clean. Cool slightly and remove from pan onto cake plate.
- Spoon glaze over cake.

GLAZE:
¾ cup butter
1 cup brown sugar
¼ cup milk
   Vanilla to taste
½ teaspoon cinnamon

- Bring butter, sugar and milk to a rolling boil. Reduce heat and cook 10 - 15 minutes, stirring occasionally to prevent scorching. Add vanilla and cinnamon.
- Cool 10 - 15 minutes.

YOGURT CAKE (Yaourtini)

YIELD:

12 -18 servings

NOTES:

This light and moist cake is a Greek favorite.

1 cup butter
2 cups sugar
6 eggs, well-beaten
1 cup yogurt
1 cup walnuts, chopped fine
2 teaspoons baking soda
2 cups flour
1 teaspoon cinnamon
1 teaspoon cloves
Walnut halves (or fresh strawberries)

- Preheat oven to 350°.

- Melt butter and cool slightly. In a mixing bowl beat butter adding sugar, then eggs, then yogurt, walnuts, soda, flour, cinnamon, cloves and beat well.

- Pour into a greased 9" x 13" baking pan. Bake in 350° oven for about one hour.

- Pour syrup over warm cake.

- Let cool and cut into squares or diamond shapes.

- Decorate each piece with walnut half (or strawberry).

SYRUP:

3 cups sugar
2 cups water
1 tablespoon lemon juice

- Boil sugar, water and lemon juice for 10 minutes.

MARMALADE CAKE

YIELDS:
Serves 12 -15

NOTES:
This wonderfully moist cake freezes for months, unfrosted, if carefully wrapped in heavy duty foil.

3/4 cup butter, softened
1 cup sugar
1 tablespoon grated orange rind
1 tablespoon vanilla
3 eggs
1 cup good quality bitter English marmalade
3 cups all-purpose flour
1 1/2 teaspoons baking soda
1 teaspoon salt
1/2 cup orange juice
1/2 cup evaporated milk
1 cup chopped nuts

- Cream the butter thoroughly. Add sugar, orange rind and vanilla. Beat until mixture is light and fluffy.

- Add eggs, one at a time, beating well after each addition. Blend in marmalade.

- Sift together flour, baking soda and salt.

- Add flour mixture to creamed mixture alternately with combined orange juice and evaporated milk. Stir in nuts.

- Stir into well-buttered 10" tube pan.

- Bake at 350° for 55 to 60 minutes. Cool in pan for 10 minutes and remove. Serve warm or cooled.

ORANGE TOPPING SAUCE:

1/3 cup orange juice
1/3 cup sugar

- Combine in sauce pan and stir over medium heat until the sugar dissolves.

- Make little holes in the surface of the cake with a skewer and spoon sauce over top.

COCONUT CREAM CAKE

YIELDS:
Serves 12

NOTES:
*Frozen coconut
retains its moisture
better than canned.*

$^1/_2$ cup shortening
$^1/_2$ cup butter
2 cups sugar
5 eggs at room temperature, separated
1 teaspoon baking soda
1 cup buttermilk
2 cups flour
1 teaspoon vanilla
2 cups grated coconut (buy frozen coconut)
   Coconut Frosting (see below)

- Preheat oven to 350°.

- Beat shortening, butter and sugar until creamy. Blend in egg yolks.

- Add baking soda to buttermilk. Stir flour and buttermilk alternately into egg mixture.

- Beat egg whites until stiff and add vanilla.

- Fold into cake mixture. Stir in 1 $^2/_3$ cups coconut.

- Bake in three 8" or 9" layer pans, greased and floured, at 350° for 30 minutes.

- Spread frosting over layers, top and sides of cake. Sprinkle remaining $^1/_3$ cup coconut on top of frosting.

COCONUT FROSTING

YIELDS:
3 cups

NOTES:
*In a hurry use this
frosting to ice a pound
cake from the bakery.*

$^1/_2$ cup butter
8 ounces cream cheese
1 pound powdered sugar
1 teaspoon vanilla
1 cup grated coconut (buy frozen coconut)
1 cup chopped pecans (or walnuts)

- Blend butter and cream cheese.

- Add sugar and vanilla and fold in coconut and nuts.

TRIFLE CHEESECAKE

YIELD:
Serves 12

NOTES:
A beautiful presentation!

CRUST:

1   package Bordeaux cookies, crushed
2   tablespoons melted butter

- Preheat oven to 325°.
- Mix and press crumbs into bottom of greased 9-inch springform pan.
- Bake at 325° for 10 minutes.

FILLING:

3   (8 ounce) packages cream cheese, softened
3/4   cup sugar
4   eggs
1/2   cup sour cream
1/2   cup whipping cream
2   tablespoons sweet sherry
1   teaspoon vanilla

- Combine cream cheese and sugar and beat until smooth.
- Add eggs, one at a time, mixing well after each addition.
- Fold in sour cream, whipping cream, sherry and vanilla. Pour over crust.
- Bake at 325° for 1 hour and 10 minutes.
- Loosen cake from rim and cool before removing rim from pan.

TOPPING:

1   (10 ounce) jar red raspberry preserves
2   Kiwi fruit, peeled and sliced
1/2   cup heavy cream, whipped
     Slivered almonds, toasted

- Heat preserves until melted. Strain to remove seeds.
- Spoon over cheesecake, spreading to the edges.
- Decorate with whipped cream and almonds, garnishing with slices of fruit.

CHOCOLATE BUTTERMILK LAYER CAKE

YIELD:

Serves 12

NOTES:

Can be prepared 1 month in advance and frozen in plastic freezer bags.

This cake is beautifully enhanced with decorative Chocolate Leaves (see page 233).

2 ½   cups cake flour
   ½   cup1 unsweetened cocoa powder
   2   teaspoons baking soda
   ¾   teaspoon salt
2 ¼   cups sugar
   1   cup unsalted butter, cut into 8 pieces, room temperature
   2   large eggs
   2   cups buttermilk
   1   teaspoon vanilla
     Chocolate Frosting (see page 251)

- Preheat oven to 350°.

- Butter three 9" round pans. Line bottoms with parchment paper, and butter the paper.

- In a food processor, place flour, cocoa, baking soda and salt. Process 5 seconds. Remove from bowl and set aside.

- Process sugar, butter and eggs until creamy, about 2 minutes.

- With machine running, add buttermilk and vanilla.

- Place dry ingredients on top of batter and process only until flour is incorporated. Scrape down sides of bowl, and do not over mix.

- Pour batter into pans. Bake at 350° about 30 minutes.

- Cool in pans. Invert onto racks. Remove paper.

- Spread Chocolate Frosting over layers, top and sides of cake.

CHOCOLATE FROSTING

6 ounces unsweetened chocolate, broken into pieces

$^1/_2$ cup unsalted butter cut into 4 pieces at room temperature

1 tablespoon vanilla

$1^1/_2$ cups sugar

1 cup whipping cream

- In a food processor add chocolate pieces. Process chocolate until ground. Add butter and vanilla and process until smooth.

- Stir sugar and cream in 8-cup glass measuring bowl. Cook on high in microwave, uncovered, for 8 minutes.

- Add chocolate mixture and stir until melted. Cover and refrigerate.

- In a food processor mix frosting until light, about 2 minutes. Scrape sides of bowl frequently.

CHEESECAKE FIGURE EIGHT

YIELD:

Serves 12

NOTES:

*The flavor of most
cheescakes is
enhanced when
prepared a day ahead.*

*A most unusual
cheesecake in that
it has no crust!*

32	ounces cream cheese
1/4	pound unsalted butter
16	ounces sour cream
1 3/4	cups sugar
2	teaspoons vanilla
1	teaspoon fresh lemon juice
2	tablespoons cornstarch
5	large eggs

All ingredients must be at room temperature.

- Preheat oven to 375°.

- In a large mixing bowl, blend all ingredients except eggs.

- When all is well blended, beat in eggs, one at a time.

- Pour into a greased 10" springform pan.

- Set filled springform pan into a larger pan. Then fill large pan half way with hot water.

- Bake in 375° oven for one hour. Turn off oven. Open oven door and let stand in the oven for one more hour.

- Remove from oven and leave at room temperature for about two hours.

- Refrigerate overnight. Unmold and garnish with fresh fruit if desired.

MOCHA ANGEL FOOD PUDDING

YIELD:
Serves 12

NOTES:
This rich dessert must be made a day ahead but is well worth the calories and well worth the effort.

4 teaspoons instant coffee
1 envelope gelatin
1 tablespoon cocoa
3/4 cup sugar
4 egg yolks, beaten
4 egg whites
   pinch of cream of tartar
   pinch of salt
2 cups heavy cream, whipped
1 Angel food cake, broken in pieces
3/4 cup toasted almonds

- Dissolve instant coffee in 1/2 cup water.
- Soften gelatin in 1/4 cup water.
- For custard, mix cocoa with 1/2 cup sugar and beat into yolks.
- Add coffee and gelatin.
- Cook slowly in a double boiler over hot water until thickened, stirring constantly.
- Add cream of tartar and salt to egg whites. Beat until stiff. Continue beating and gradually add the remaining sugar.
- Fold egg whites into cooled custard. Fold in whipped cream.
- To assemble, put a layer of the cake in a large angel food cake pan, cover with custard mixture and repeat layering until pan is full.
- Refrigerate for 12 or more hours.
- A few hours before serving unmold and cover with mocha whipped cream. Refrigerate.
- Just before serving sprinkle with almonds.

MOCHA WHIPPED CREAM

1 cup heavy cream
3 tablespoons powdered sugar
1 tablespoon instant coffee
2 tablespoons crème de cacao or Kahlua (or 1 teaspoon vanilla)

- Beat all ingredients together until whipped.

FLOWER POTS

YIELD:

1 serving (multiply as needed)

NOTES:

This is not necessarily a children's party dessert. Adults are known to ooh and aah.

1 (3 ¹/₂-inch) clay flower pot (one for each guest)
   Pound cake, sliced ¹/₂ inch thick
   Ice cream (any flavor except fruit)
   Plastic drinking straws, cut into 2" lengths
   Fudge sauce, cooled
   Small edible fresh flowers

- In a large stock pot, boil clay pots for 25 minutes to sterilize. Remove, cool and dry.

- Cut a round piece of pound cake to cover holes in bottom of pots.

- Pack to within ¹/₂ inch of top of pot with ice cream.

- Push cut plastic straws into ice cream until even with top of pots.

- Cover ice cream with fudge sauce.

- Keep in freezer until just before serving.

- Put a fresh daisy or miniature rose or pansy or any small flower into straw.

PEPPERMINT-CHOCOLATE ICE CREAM TORTE

YIELD:
Serves 12 - 14

NOTES:
This dessert must be prepared a day ahead and frozen.

Any flavor of ice cream is great, provided it marries well with peppermint.

1   (9 ounce) package chocolate wafer cookies, crushed in blender
3/4   cup unsalted butter, melted
2   quarts peppermint ice cream, or mint chocolate chip, or chocolate mint, softened slightly
1   cup crushed peppermint candy
    Chocolate Truffle Sauce (see below)

- Preheat oven to 375°.
- Butter a 9" springform pan.
- Mix crumbs with melted butter until moist.
- Press mixture in bottom of pan and one inch up the sides.
- Bake crust for 10 minutes and cool completely.
- Fill crust with ice cream, and put in freezer overnight.
- To serve, unmold torte onto serving plate. Drizzle with chocolate sauce and sprinkle candy over top.

CHOCOLATE TRUFFLE SAUCE

YIELD:
Makes about 2 cups

1/2   cup whipping cream
1/2   cup unsalted butter, cut into pieces
3   ounces semi-sweet chocolate, chopped
1   teaspoon vanilla

- In a heavy, medium size saucepan barely bring cream and butter to a simmer. Remove from heat.
- Add semi-sweet chocolate and vanilla and whisk until smooth.
- Can be prepared 2 weeks ahead.
- Before using, heat over medium heat, stirring frequently.

HOT FUDGE SAUCE

YIELD:
Makes 1 1/2 cups

NOTES:
This can also be chocolate fondue. Use fresh fruit and poundcake for dipping.

7   ounces bittersweet chocolate, broken in pieces (not unsweetened)
2   teaspoons instant coffee granules
2   teaspoons boiling water
1   tablespoon coffee liqueur
1/2   cup plus 6 tablespoons sweet butter

- Place chocolate, coffee granules and water in top of double boiler.
- Slowly cook until only small pieces of chocolate remain.
- Add liqueur and butter and cook until butter melts.
- Remove from heat and stir until sauce is smooth.
- Serve warm over ice cream.

HOT COFFEE SAUCE

YIELD:
1 3/4 cups

NOTES:
Delicious served hot over vanilla or chocolate ice cream.

1   cup half and half
1   cup milk
6   tablespoons very strong black coffee (or 1 1/2 tablespoons instant coffee granules)
1   egg yolk
1/4   cup sugar

- Heat the half and half and milk with coffee very slowly.
- Beat the yolk and sugar vigorously until pale and thick, approximately 8 minutes.
- Continue beating while pouring a very thin stream of the hot cream mixture into egg mixture.
- Return mixture to pan. Stir over heat until thickened. Strain.

Professional Chefs

Will Henry Stevens (1881-1949)
Abstraction, 1938
Oil on canvas
Gift of John W. Hess in memory of Barbara Hess

Considered the South's major geometric Abstractionist, Will Henry Stevens
taught from 1921 to 1948 at the Newcomb School of Art at Tulane University
in New Orleans. He spent his summers in the mountains of North Carolina
where he was inspired by the natural beauty of the landscape and rural architecture.

CRANBERRY-GLAZED BRIE

From: Catherine McGregor Faver

YIELD:
Serves 20

NOTES:
Well traveled chef Catherine Faver enjoys combining international delicacies with traditional southern favorites.

Buy cranberries when available and store in freezer.

1 (2.2 pound) wheel of brie (8 inches in diameter)
Crackers
Apple and pear slices

CRANBERRY MARMALADE:

3 cups raw cranberries
$^3/_4$ cup firmly packed brown sugar
$^1/_3$ cup dried currants
$^1/_3$ cup water
$^1/_8$ teaspoon dry mustard
$^1/_8$ teaspoon ground allspice
$^1/_8$ teaspoon ground cardamom
$^1/_8$ teaspoon ground cloves
$^1/_8$ teaspoon ground ginger

- Combine all marmalade ingredients in heavy non-aluminum saucepan.
- Cook over medium heat until most of the berries pop, about 5 minutes, stirring frequently.
- Cool to room temperature. (Can be prepared 3 days ahead. Cover and refrigerate.)
- Using sharp knife, cut circle in top rind of cheese, leaving $^1/_2$ inch border of rind. Carefully remove center circle of rind from cheese. Do not cut through side rind.
- Place cheese in 8-inch diameter ceramic baking dish or on cookie sheet lined with foil.
- Spread cranberry marmalade over cheese. (Can be prepared 6 hours ahead. Cover and refrigerate. Bring cheese to room temperature before continuing).
- Preheat oven to 300°. Bake cheese until soft, about 12 minutes.
- Set cheese on large platter. Cool slightly. Surround with crackers and fruit.
- Serve warm or at room temperature.

NEW POTATOES WITH ROASTED RED PEPPER SPREAD

From: Hilda Cameron and Katharine Sullivan

YIELD:
Serves 35

NOTES:

East meets West in the unique blending of styles of California Culinary Academy chef Katharine Sullivan and Peter Kump's New York School of Culinary Arts chef Hilda Cameron.

Roasted Red Pepper Spread can be served with crackers instead of potatoes.

2   yellow bell peppers
2   red bell peppers
1   medium onion, sliced
    Olive oil
2   heads garlic, cut in half
1/4 teaspoon dry basil
1/4 teaspoon dry oregano
1   tablespoon balsamic vinegar
    Salt and freshly ground pepper to taste
4   ounces goat cheese, crumbled
2   pounds small new potatoes (size b)

- Roast peppers by placing on grill or in high oven, turning frequently, until skins turn black, or skin loosens from meat. When finished, place in a bowl and cover with plastic wrap to steam. Let sit about 5 minutes. Remove skin, seed and dice.
- Toss onion slices with salt and pepper in enough oil to coat.
- Roast onions by placing on grill or in a sauté pan, cooking until golden brown. Dice.
- Place garlic halves cut side down in a glass oven-proof dish.
- Cover bottom of dish with water and sprinkle with 1 tablespoon oil. Bake at 300° for 30 minutes or until soft. Cool. Remove garlic cloves from skin.
- Cut potatoes in half. Trim opposite end so potato will sit flat. Place on a greased sheet pan (cut side up).
- Sprinkle with salt and cover with foil. Place in preheated 400° oven. Bake for 1 hour or until tender. Cool.
- With a melon baller, scoop out a small portion of the potato. Chill until ready to fill.
- To prepare roasted red pepper spread, mix roasted peppers, onions, garlic, basil, oregano and goat cheese. Mix well.
- When ready to serve, fill potatoes with red pepper spread.

BAKED STUFFED ARTICHOKE
WITH AÏOLI

From: Landfall Club House

YIELD:

Serves 2

NOTES:

This private club sets a standard for elegant international cuisine in North Carolina.

Aïoli is a flavorful garlic mayonnaise from the south of France.

Aïoli can also be served as a popular accompaniment with vegetables, fish, or meats.

2 medium artichokes
Salted water
1 lemon, cut in quarters
Croutons
Parmesan cheese, shredded
Italian vinaigrette

- Cut off the stems of the artichokes so they will sit flat.
- Bring water to a boil and add lemon quarters.
- Submerge the artichokes in boiling salted water for 45 minutes, or until leaves are tender.
- Drain and cool.
- Stand artichokes on cookie sheet and spread open the leaves.
- Stuff the leaves randomly with croutons, Parmesan cheese and Italian vinaigrette.
- Bake at 350° until warm inside.
- Serve with aïoli for dipping.

AÏOLI:

2 egg yolks
8 ounces olive oil
$^1/_2$ teaspoon fresh garlic
$^1/_2$ teaspoon mustard
Salt and freshly ground pepper to taste
$^1/_2$ teaspoon lemon juice

- In the food processor, purée yolks until light and smooth.
- Slowly drizzle in olive oil until mixture looks like mayonnaise.
- Add the rest of the ingredients and purée until smooth. Adjust flavor.
- Set aïoli aside.

TRAILS END MEATBALLS

From: Trails End Steak House

YIELD:
100 meatballs

NOTES:
A traditional steak house overlooking Wilmington's unspoiled Intracoastal Waterway.

Make ahead and freeze.

Preparation time 30 minutes.

5   pounds ground beef
1   tablespoon granulated garlic
2   tablespoons hot pepper sauce
2   tablespoons soy sauce
2   tablespoons Worcestershire sauce
    Dash red pepper
2 ½   tablespoons black pepper
1   onion, finely chopped (optional)
1   small jar jalapeño relish
    Sweet and sour sauce (or spaghetti sauce)

- Mix together all ingredients and shape into small meatballs.

- Bake in 375° oven until brown.

- Drain and serve with sweet and sour sauce (or your favorite spaghetti sauce).

- Serve in chafing dish with toothpicks.

HEARTY TORTELLINI-VEGETABLE SOUP

From: Temptations

YIELD:
Serves 6

NOTES:

A gourmet store offering casual dining and an international selection of foods.

Truly a meal in a dish.

Easy to prepare vegetables ahead, reheat and combine with tortellini just before serving.

3 cups quartered small mushrooms

1 cup chopped onions

1 cup chopped carrots

1 cup chopped zucchini

1 tablespoon plus 1 teaspoon olive (or vegetable oil)

2 small garlic cloves, minced

4 cups thoroughly washed, drained and steamed spinach leaves

3 cups canned stewed tomatoes

2 cups chicken broth

2 tablespoon chopped parsley

2 tablespoons chopped fresh dill (or basil)

56 frozen tortellini

- In a 4-quart microwavable casserole, combine mushrooms, onions, carrots, zucchini, oil and garlic. Stir to coat.

- Cover and microwave on high for 6 minutes. Turn and continue for 4 minutes more.

- Add remaining ingredients except tortellini. Cover and microwave on high for 6 minutes.

- Boil tortellini according to package directions. Mix with microwaved ingredients.

- Correct seasonings.

IMPERIAL CHICKEN

From: Szechuan 132 and Szechuan 130

YIELD:

Serves 2 over steamed rice

NOTES:

This is delicious, and works well in the home kitchen.

An option is to season with chili powder to make spicy.

1	egg white
1	tablespoon light soy sauce
2	chicken legs, boned and cut in 1 ½" cubes
½	teaspoon sesame oil
2	cups vegetable oil
3	pieces Szechuan dried peppers
¼	teaspoon ground ginger
3	cloves fresh garlic, minced
1	teaspoon light soy sauce
1	teaspoon vinegar
½	teaspoon sugar
2	tablespoons cornstarch dissolved in 2 tablespoons water
1	green bell pepper, chopped
½	red bell pepper, chopped
10 - 15	pieces baby corn
½	head broccoli, steamed

- Combine egg white and 1 tablespoon light soy sauce, and toss chicken pieces in the mixture to coat.

- Heat sesame and vegetable oils in wok to 280°, and deep fry chicken until golden brown. Remove with slotted spoon.

- Reserve 2 teaspoons oil, discarding the rest.

- Stir-fry Szechuan peppers in the reserved oil for 2 seconds, add ginger and garlic for another 2 seconds, then add 1 teaspoon light soy sauce, vinegar and sugar.

- Add cornstarch solution and stir until thickened.

- For added color, stir in bell peppers and baby corn.

- Garnish with steamed broccoli.

ROAST RACK OF AUSTRALIAN LAMB
With Poached Sweet Carrots and Zucchini Farcis

From: Christian Clements

YIELD:
Serves 2 - 4

NOTES:
Chef Clements has served this many times to great success at the Figure Eight Island Yacht Club.

1   quart veal stock
1   cup red wine
2   large shallots, chopped
1   sprig of fresh thyme, minced
1   clove garlic, minced
$^1/_2$ cup grainy mustard
1   green zucchini, not less than 7 inches in length
1   medium carrot, not less than 7 inches in length
2   tablespoons olive oil, divided
1   (23 ounce) Australian rack of lamb, frenched
1   teaspoon salt
1   teaspoon coarsely ground pepper
$^1/_2$ pound salted butter

- In a saucepan, combine veal stock and red wine, turn to high flame and reduce by half.
- In a small bowl, combine shallots, thyme, garlic and mustard, adding to stock.
- With large boning knife, whittle the carrot down to one-quarter inch in diameter.
- Slice the zucchini in half lengthwise, hollowing out the center to accommodate the carrot.
- Place the carrot in the hollowed zucchini, and poach in veal stock for two minutes. Remove and cool with cold running water so that vegetables remain firm.
- Brush stuffed zucchini with 1 tablespoon olive oil, and insert gently into loin of lamb, being careful not to break it.
- In a large saucepan, heat remaining oil over a high flame.
- Coat lamb with salt and pepper to taste and quickly brown in oil.
- Place in a 400° oven for 30 minutes.
- Add reduced veal stock and cook for 15 minutes.
- Add butter to hot roast, remove lamb from oven, and slice into chops, showing stuffing.
- Spread sauce evenly on serving plate and fan the lamb slices over it.

SOUR CREAM HORSERADISH SAUCE

From: The Surf Club

YIELD:
Makes 1 ½ cups

NOTES:
A very good accompaniment for smoked fish. Can be used in lieu of mayonnaise on a meat sandwich.

1	cup sour cream
¼	cup mayonnaise
2	tablespoons prepared horseradish
1	tablespoon Dijon mustard
2	tablespoons honey
	Salt and pepper to taste
4	drops hot pepper sauce
½	teaspoon Worcestershire sauce

- Mix all ingredients in stainless steel bowl with wire whisk until smooth.

- Adjust seasonings to personal taste.

CUMBERLAND SAUCE

From: The Surf Club

YIELD:
Makes 7 cups

NOTES:
Serve with pork, poultry or game.

1	quart red currant jelly
4	tablespoons blanched, chopped shallots
8	tablespoons blanched orange and lemon zest
4	teaspoons dry mustard
2	cups port wine
1	cup orange juice
½	cup lemon juice
	Cayenne pepper to taste
	Ginger to taste

- Combine all ingredients in a pot and simmer for 15 minutes.

- Cool and refrigerate.

WHARF - STYLE MUSSELS

From: The Pilot House

YIELD:

Serves 8

NOTES:

To make a richer dish, reduce the cooking liquid and top with ¹/₂ cup heavy cream.

To clean mussels: Wipe your sink with a clean cloth, rinse, and fill with cold tap water. Place rinsed mussels in water and sprinkle with a handful of corn meal. The mussels will intake the corn meal and disgorge any sand or grit that they might contain. If a mussel is open, tap it lightly against the counter-top. If it closes, it is alive and usable. If it does not close, discard it. Leave mussels in the cold water for about one hour. Remove the coarse, fringe-like beard by pulling gently. The mussels are now ready for use.

¹/₄	pound butter
1	cup finely diced shallots
1	cup finely diced white onion
¹/₂	cup peeled minced carrot
¹/₂	cup minced celery
3	cups dry white wine (Sauvignon Blanc, Pinot Grigio, or other)
1	teaspoon salt
1	teaspoon freshly ground pepper
8	quarts debearded mussels
¹/₂	cup chopped parsley

- In a large stock pot, melt the butter and stir in the shallots, onion, carrot and celery.
- Allow to cook briefly without browning the vegetables at all.
- Stir in the white wine, salt and pepper.
- When the mixture has reached the simmering point, add the mussels, cover and steam approximately 8 minutes, stirring quickly once or twice.
- When most of the mussels have popped open, they are done. The few that have not opened will do so from the residual heat.
- Toss in the parsley and serve hot in a broad shallow bowl with some of the cooking liquid poured over the top.
- Serve with crisp sourdough or a baguette.

VONGOLE AL FORNO CON PANCETTA

(Roasted Clams with Bacon)

From: Etrusca

YIELD:
Serves 2

NOTES:
Spontaneous chef Mike Stanley works wonders creating exotic meals with whatever is in the pantry.

CLAMS:

12 fresh littleneck clams
Salt to taste
Cornmeal or all-purpose flour

- Place clams in a bowl of cool water with a few big pinches of salt and a handful of cornmeal or flour.

- Leave in refrigerator for at least 3 hours or overnight so the clams will purge themselves of sand and other foreign matter.

- Scrub the clams to remove exterior dirt, and place them in a bowl of very hot water for 5 - 10 minutes to facilitate opening them.

- Meanwhile, preheat broiler. In a mixing bowl, combine all topping ingredients and mix well.

- Working over a bowl to catch any clam juice, insert a clam knife between clam's shell.

- Open clam, thrusting blade toward muscle on base of shell.

- Detach flesh from shell cavity to make it easier to lift out when eating. Leave the whole clam meat in one of its shells, discarding other shell. Repeat with all the clams.

TOPPING:

1 tablespoon extra-virgin olive oil
1 small clove garlic, finely chopped
1 tablespoon fine dried bread crumbs
1 tablespoon chopped roasted red sweet pepper
1 teaspoon chopped fresh Italian parsley
2 tablespoons finely chopped pancetta or cooked bacon

- Mix all ingredients together except wine, clam juices and lemon wedges.

TO ASSEMBLE:

Reserved clam juices
Dry white wine for sprinkling
1 lemon, cut into wedges, for garnish

- Spoon an equal amount of topping on each clam, drizzling a little clam juice from the bowl on top, and sprinkling with a little wine to keep clams moist and prevent them from burning.
- Place clams in a flame-proof baking dish and place dish 9 inches away from broiler.
- Broil about 6 minutes, watching carefully to be sure topping does not burn. Serve hot with lemon wedges.

TOMATO BASIL RISOTTO WITH CLAMS AND MUSSELS

From: Clarence Foster's

YIELD:
Serves 8 - 10

NOTES:
Coastal Carolinians enjoy an abundance of fresh shellfish. This island restaurant takes advantage of the bounty of our region.

6 ounces butter
2 medium onions, chopped
3 cloves garlic, minced
20 ounces Arborio rice
10 ounces white wine
2 (14 1/2 ounce) cans chicken stock
1 (32 ounce) can tomato juice
   Salt and freshly ground pepper
30 Clams, cleaned
30 Mussels, cleaned
1 pint cherry tomatoes, or 12 Roma tomatoes, sliced
   Fresh or dried basil

- In a saucepan, melt butter and sauté onion and garlic until onion is translucent.

- Add rice and wine and simmer, stirring, until wine is absorbed (about 5 minutes).

- Alternating between chicken stock and tomato juice, 1/2 cup at a time, add to rice, stirring frequently, until all liquid is absorbed. Arborio rice should be done in 30 - 35 minutes.

- Season with salt and pepper.

- In a separate pan, place clams and mussels with enough water to cover bottom of pan generously. Cover and steam to open.

- When shells begin to open, toss in tomatoes.

- In 8 or 10 individual pasta bowls, place risotto, clams, mussels and tomatoes. Divide juice among the bowls and garnish with fresh or dried basil.

SZECHUAN CRISPY SHRIMP

From: Szechuan 132 and Szechuan 130

YIELD:
Serves 2

NOTES:
Owner Joseph Hou combines the finest Asian recipes with the freshest of North Carolina's native ingredients to create a memorable menu.

12 jumbo prawns (or shrimps)
$^3/_4$ cup cornstarch
$^1/_4$ cup flour
4 cups vegetable oil
$^1/_2$ cup chicken broth
1 $^1/_2$ tablespoons ketchup
2 teaspoons sugar
2 teaspoons white vinegar
$^1/_8$ teaspoon salt
1 tablespoon sesame seeds
1 head steamed broccoli

- Remove the heads and shells from prawns, leaving the tails.

- Devein, rinse and drain.

- Place the prawns in the marinade for 15 minutes.

- Coat the prawns with cornstarch and flour combination.

- Heat vegetable oil to 280°, and deep fry prawns until golden brown. Drain.

- Combine broth, ketchup, sugar, vinegar and salt in a wok and bring to a boil. Pour sauce over prawns and sprinkle with sesame seeds.

- Garnish with steamed broccoli.

MARINADE:

$^1/_3$ egg white
1 tablespoon cornstarch
1 teaspoon cooking wine
1 teaspoon sesame oil
$^1/_2$ teaspoon sugar
$^1/_4$ teaspoon salt
$^1/_8$ teaspoon pepper

- Mix all marinade ingredients.

SAUTÉED GROUPER
WITH SHIITAKE MUSHROOMS

From: Gardenia's

YIELD:
Serves 4

NOTES:
Chef Gale Tolan is a master at combining foods with unusual flavors. This is one of Gardenia's most popular dishes.

1	cup flour
	Salt and pepper to taste
3	medium eggs
$1/2$	cup milk
4	7 - 8 ounce grouper fillets
4	tablespoons peanut oil
3	tablespoons unsalted butter
2	tablespoons shallots, finely minced
16	Shiitake mushrooms, stems removed
1	(14 ounce) can artichoke hearts, drained and cut in halves
1	lemon

- Season flour with salt and pepper.

- In small mixing bowl, beat eggs and mix with milk.

- Coat grouper fillets in flour. Dip in egg mixture.

- Heat peanut oil over medium high heat.

- Place fish in oil and lightly brown on both sides.

- Place in oven-proof pan and cook in 375° oven until done all the way through (approximately 8 - 10 minutes).

- While the fish is finishing, pour off the peanut oil.

- Add the butter to skillet. Sauté shallots for 2 minutes, add Shiitake mushrooms and cook 3 - 4 minutes.

- Add artichoke hearts and continue to cook until artichokes are hot.

- Shake skillet several times to mix ingredients and to eliminate sticking.

- During the last minute of cooking, squeeze lemon juice into skillet. Salt and pepper to taste.

- Remove grouper from the oven and place on serving plate. Top with sautéed vegetables.

PECAN ENCRUSTED SALMON

From: Jerry's Food, Wine & Spirits

YIELD:

Serves 6

NOTES:

Chef Jerry Rouse has created a neighborhood restaurant noted for fine dining in a warm atmosphere.

Always start with the freshest fish.

6   (8 ounce) portions of salmon, skinned, fileted, pin bones removed
    Flour for dusting
3   cups medium chopped pecans
1   teaspoon curry powder
    Salt and freshly ground pepper (or lemon pepper) to taste
1   tablespoon chopped parsley
    Egg wash (whole egg beaten with small amount of water)

- Lightly coat salmon with flour.

- Mix pecans, curry, salt, pepper and parsley.

- Dip salmon into egg wash, then directly into pecan mixture.

- Place fish in baking dish in a 400° oven for 15 minutes.

- Serve with the following sauce on the side.

SAUCE:

2   cups fish or chicken stock
2   tablespoons chopped fresh tarragon (or dill)
2   tablespoons minced shallots
2   tablespoons heavy cream
2   tablespoons butter
    White wine to taste

- Add herbs and shallots to stock and reduce for 10 minutes.

- Stir in cream, butter and wine.

GAMBERI E FAGIOLE
CANNELLINI ALLA TOSCANA

(Tuscan-Style Shrimp and Cannellini Beans)

From: Etrusca

YIELD:

Serves 4

NOTES:

If you're pressed for time, this hearty dish can be made with 2 cups canned white beans with their liquid, and 1 cup canned plum tomatoes, drained, seeded and chopped.

1	cup dried cannellini (or Great Northern beans)
1	clove garlic, unpeeled, bruised
1	bay leaf
1	pound ripe plum tomatoes, peeled
3/4	pound shrimp, peeled and deveined
6	tablespoons extra-virgin olive oil, divided
2	large cloves garlic, finely chopped, plus 1 clove garlic, bruised
2	tablespoons fresh basil leaves, torn into small pieces, or chopped, plus whole leaves for garnish
2	teaspoons chopped fresh Italian parsley
1 1/8	teaspoons salt, or to taste
1/4	teaspoon freshly ground pepper, or to taste

- Soak and cook the beans as directed, adding the unpeeled garlic clove and bay leaf to the cooking water.

- Drain beans when they are just tender and reserve 1/2 cup of the cooking liquid. You wll have about 2 cups cooked beans. Discard garlic and bay leaf.

- Cut peeled fresh tomatoes in half crosswise. Remove and discard their seeds, then cut into medium dice. You will have about 1 cup.

- Dry the shrimp with a cotton kitchen towel.

- Heat 4 tablespoons olive oil in a large skillet and add the shrimp.
- Sauté until the shrimp are almost cooked, about 2 minutes on each side.
- Add chopped garlic, torn or chopped basil, parsley, beans and the reserved liquid.
- Season with salt and pepper to taste and heat through, about 2 minutes.
- In another pan, heat 1 tablespoon of remaining oil with bruised garlic clove and sauté until lightly brown.
- Add tomatoes and cook for 1 minute. Remove and discard garlic.
- Stir tomatoes into shrimp and beans.
- Drizzle remaining olive oil over dish. Garnish with whole basil leaves. Serve hot or warm.

GLORIOUS GROUPER

From: Sarah Hedgpeth, Caterer

YIELD:
Serves 6 - 8

NOTES:
A chef of many hats, Sarah Hedgpeth is a noted restauranteur, caterer, and food aficionado.

3 pounds fresh grouper fillets
   Salt and lemon pepper
1 tablespoon light oil
1 large onion, chopped
1/2 cup chives, chopped
1 cup fresh mushrooms, sliced
1 cup dry white wine
2 tablespoons butter
2 tablespoons lemon juice
2 lemons, thinly sliced
1 tablespoon fresh dill, finely cut
1 tablespoon parsley, chopped

- Season fish with sea salt and lemon pepper.
- Brush oil over ovenproof baking dish.
- Arrange onions, chives and mushrooms on bottom of dish. Sprinkle with salt and lemon pepper.
- Place fish fillets on top and pour wine over.
- Brush tops of fish with combined butter and lemon juice.
- Top with lemon slices and sprinkle with dill and parsley.
- Bake in preheated 350° oven 20 to 25 minutes or until fish is white and flaky.
- Serve with dill sauce on the side.

DILL SAUCE:

1 egg, well-beaten
1 teaspoon salt
4 teaspoons lemon juice
2 teaspoons grated onion
2 tablespoons finely cut fresh dill
1 1/2 cups sour cream
1 teaspoon sugar
   Pinch white pepper
1/8 teaspoon curry powder

- Add all ingredients to beaten egg and blend well.
- Chill.

PASTA SHELLS WITH SCALLOPS AND BASIL

From: Etrusca

YIELD:
Serves 4

NOTES:

This Italian restaurant combines the freshest seafood of the Carolina shores with the robust flavors and flair of Rome.

Orange and tomato flavors...a new twist with scallops.

10	ounces medium pasta shells
2	tablespoons cornstarch
1	pound sea scallops, halved crosswise if very large
2	tablespoons olive oil
2	cloves garlic, minced
$^1/_2$	cup sliced scallions
$^3/_4$	pound tomatoes, coarsely chopped
3	tablespoons chopped fresh basil
3	tablespoons orange juice
1	teaspoon grated orange zest
$^3/_4$	teaspoon salt

- Heat a large pot of water to boiling and cook pasta shells until just tender. Drain well.

- Meanwhile, spread the cornstarch on a plate. Dredge scallops in cornstarch, shaking off excess.

- Heat oil over medium heat until hot but not smoking.

- Add scallops and cook, stirring, until lightly golden, about 2 minutes.

- Add garlic and scallions and cook, stirring frequently, until garlic is tender, about 2 minutes.

- With a slotted spoon, transfer scallop mixture to a plate.

- Add tomatoes, basil, orange juice, zest and salt to pan and cook until slightly thickened, about 4 minutes.

- Stir in scallop mixture and cook until scallops are just opaque, about 1 minute longer.

- Transfer mixture to a large bowl, add the pasta shells and toss to combine.

- Spoon into 4 shallow bowls and serve.

SHRIMP AND GRITS

From: Crook's By The River

YIELD:
Serves 4

Notes:
A famous recipe from one of the "New South's" notable restaurants using traditional ingredients to develop an exciting new dish.

1	pound medium size shrimp, peeled
6	slices bacon
	Olive oil
2	cups sliced fresh mushrooms
1	cup sliced scallions
1	large clove garlic, crushed
4	teaspoons fresh lemon juice
	Dash of hot red pepper sauce
2	tablespoons chopped fresh parsley
	Salt and freshly ground pepper to taste
1	recipe Cheese Grits, hot (see page 279)

- Rinse shrimp and pat dry on paper towels.

- Fry and crumble the bacon and set aside.

- Add enough oil to the bacon fat to make a thin layer.

- Heat over medium high heat until the fat is quite hot. Add the shrimp and cook until they begin to color.

- Add the mushrooms and sauté, stirring frequently, about 4 minutes.

- Sprinkle with the scallions and bacon, then add the garlic.

- Season with the lemon juice, hot red pepper sauce, parsley, salt and pepper.

- Divide the grits among 4 warm plates.

- Spoon shrimp mixture over top and serve immediately.

CHEESE GRITS

YIELD:

Serves 4

NOTES:

*Cheese Grits can be
served for dinner with
grilled fish or for
breakfast with eggs.*

1   cup grits

$^1/_4$ teaspoon ground white pepper
    Pinch of cayenne

1   cup shredded sharp Cheddar cheese, or more, to taste

2   tablespoons butter
    Salt to taste

- Prepare grits according to the directions on the box.

- When fully cooked, remove from heat and add the rest of the ingredients.

- Stir till smooth.

FETTUCINI WITH FRESH SALMON

From: Etrusca

YIELD:

Serves 4

NOTES:

Serve with a leafy green salad with red onion, cucumber and cherry tomatoes tossed with a reduced-fat herb vinaigrette.

1 cup reduced-sodium chicken broth, defatted
1/3 cup dry white wine
3/4 pound skinned salmon fillets, any visible bones removed, cut into 1/2" thick slices
4 scallions, minced
1 red bell pepper, diced
1 tablespoon no-salt added tomato paste
1 tablespoon fresh lemon juice
1/4 cup snipped fresh dill
1 1/2 teaspoons cornstarch
5 ounces fresh fettucini
5 ounces fresh spinach fettucini

- Start heating a large pot of water to boiling for the pasta.
- In a large skillet combine the broth and wine and bring to a boil over high heat.
- Reduce to a simmer, add the salmon, cover and cook until the salmon is just opaque, about 4 minutes.
- With a slotted spoon transfer the salmon to a plate.
- Add scallions and bell pepper to the pan and simmer, uncovered, until the bell pepper is tender, about 3 minutes.
- Stir in the tomato paste and lemon juice. Simmer until the flavors are blended, about 1 minute. Stir in dill.
- In a cup combine the cornstarch and 1 tablespoon of water and stir to blend.
- Bring the broth mixture to a boil over medium high heat, stir in the cornstarch mixture. Cook, stirring constantly, until mixture is slightly thickened, about 1 minute.
- Reduce to a simmer, add the salmon and cook until salmon is just heated through, about 30 seconds.
- Remove from heat and stir in the sour cream.
- Meanwhile, cook the fettucini in the boiling water until just tender. Drain well.
- Transfer the fettucini to a large bowl, add the salmon mixture and toss gently to combine. Spoon pasta mixture into 4 shallow bowls and serve.

SCALLOP LASAGNA

From: Caffe Phoenix

YIELD:
Serves 4 - 6

NOTES:
Debra and Michael Caliva gave birth to this restaurant where the "young and trendy" meet the "established" for a delightful repast.

2 pounds small scallops
$1/3$ cup butter, divided
1 cup chopped scallions
2 - 3 garlic cloves, minced
$1/4$ teaspoon thyme leaves
$1/3$ cup flour
1 cup chicken broth
1 cup whipping cream
$1/2$ cup dry white wine (or vermouth)
$1/2$ pound lasagna noodles
$1/2$ pound shredded Swiss cheese

- Rinse and drain scallops (if large ones, cut into half-inch pieces).

- Melt 1 tablespoon butter in frying pan, add scallions, garlic, thyme and sauté for one minute.

- Add scallops and sauté until they are opaque.

- Pour scallops into strainer over a bowl, reserving liquid, and drain 20 - 30 minutes.

- In the same pan melt remaining butter, add flour and stir until golden, remove from heat and smoothly mix in broth, cream and wine. Return to a boil, stirring, and set aside.

- Cook lasagna noodles al dente (if using fresh pasta sheets, do not pre-cook pasta - make sure to cover with sauce completely so dough does not dry out).

- Rinse cooked noodles with cold water and set aside.

- Cook scallop juice until reduced to 2 tablespoons and mix into cream sauce.

- Butter a deep rectangular pan. Alternate layers: 1) noodles, 2) sauce, 3) scallops, 4) scallions, 5) cheese. Finish with a layer of noodles, cover with sauce and sprinkle with cheese.

- Cover with lid or foil. Bake at 350° for 20 to 30 minutes. Allow to "set up" at least 15 minutes before cutting.

PASTA ESTIVI

From: Caffe Phoenix

YIELD:
Serves 4 - 6

NOTES:
*Do not attempt this recipe
with winter tomatoes or
dried herbs. It is simply
not the same.*

4   large ripe summer tomatoes, seeded and chopped
8   scallions, sliced very thin
2   cloves garlic, minced
8   tablespoons extra virgin olive oil
1/2   cup chopped fresh basil
2   tablespoons chopped garlic chives
     Salt and freshly ground pepper to taste
1   pound macaroni (It's fun to mix shapes.)
1   cup freshly grated Parmesan cheese

- Toss tomatoes, scallions, garlic, olive oil, basil, garlic chives, salt and pepper to taste.

- Allow to sit for at least 20 minutes for flavors to combine.

- Cook macaroni al dente and drain.

- While pasta is still very hot, toss with tomato mixture.

- Add Parmesan and toss. Garnish with more Parmesan and fresh basil leaves.

ANGEL HAIR RENAISSANCE

From: Giuseppe Viola

YIELD:
Serves 2

NOTES:
With true Italian flair, chef Giuseppe Viola proves the "Renaissance Man" is not extinct.

1 tablespoon chopped onion
1 tablespoon olive oil
2 cups sliced mushrooms
1/4 cup dry white wine
1 teaspoon chopped parsley
   Salt and freshly ground pepper
2 tablespoons pesto sauce
4 ounces tomato sauce
8 ounces angel hair pasta, cooked

- Sauté onion in olive oil in a large frying pan until golden brown.

- Add mushrooms and wine and continue to sauté for about 4 minutes.

- Add parsley, salt and pepper, pesto sauce and tomato sauce.

- Simmer for about 5 minutes, stirring occasionally.

- Add angel hair pasta and toss well.

- Serve with Parmesan cheese on top.

BOW-TIE PASTA WITH
CHICKEN ANDOUILLE SAUSAGE

From: Carolina's

YIELD:
Serves 4

NOTES:
Carolina's is a restaurant known for its unique blending of a variety of tastes.

2   tablespoons olive oil
2   cloves garlic, minced
1   medium onion, sliced
1   pound chicken tenders
1   pound andouille sausage, sliced
½   cup sun-dried tomatoes
1   cup cream
½   cup grated Romano cheese
    Salt and freshly ground pepper
¾   pound bow-tie pasta
    Parsley, chopped, for garnish

- Sauté garlic and onions in olive oil until translucent.

- Add chicken, sausage and sun-dried tomatoes. Cook until chicken is almost done.

- Add cream and cheese and cook until thickened.

- Add salt and pepper to taste.

- Toss mixture with bow-tie pasta.

- Garnish with chopped parsley and serve.

MUSHROOM FLAN

From: Culinarily Yours

YIELD:
Serves 20 - 25

Notes:

Owners Sharon and Chef Todd Brenner combine an innovative flair for style in each of their elegantly rich creations.

$^1/_2$ pound melted butter, divided
8 cloves garlic, minced
6 shallots, minced
5 pounds button mushrooms, sliced
1 pound assorted mushrooms (Portobello, shiitake, etc.), sliced
1 pint heavy cream
1 pound phyllo dough
$^1/_2$ cup freshly grated Parmesan cheese
$^1/_4$ cup fresh chives, chopped

- In half the melted butter, sauté garlic and shallots until golden.

- Reduce heat to medium, add mushrooms and cook, stirring, until soft.

- Blend in cream and cook sauce for 15 minutes.

- In a large buttered baking dish, arrange 3 layers of 4 phyllo sheets, buttering each layer, in a diagonal, off-set pattern.

- Add mushroom mixture and garnish by sprinkling Parmesan and chives on top.

- Criss-cross top with any left-over phyllo.

- Bake at 350° until pie is golden-brown.

SQUASH CASSEROLE

From: Thelma Hodges

YIELD:
Serves 12

NOTES:
Not a holiday has gone by in old Wilmington homes that chef Thelma Hodges' "tried and true" creations have not been on the table.

5 pounds yellow squash
$^{1}/_{2}$ cup butter
2 $^{1}/_{2}$ cups onions, sliced
Salt and pepper to taste
4 eggs, beaten
1 cup milk
1 cup bread crumbs
$^{1}/_{2}$ pound Cheddar cheese, grated

- Wash and slice squash.
- In a large saucepan melt the butter and cook squash and onions together until tender.
- Season to taste with salt and pepper.
- Mix beaten eggs and milk.
- To the squash mixture, add bread crumbs and egg-milk combination.
- Place in buttered casserole and top with grated cheese.
- Bake at 350° about 30 minutes.

WILD MUSHROOM AND SPINACH STRUDEL

From: Clarence Foster's

YIELD:
Serves 6

NOTES:
The Smoked Chipotle Coulis accompanying the Strudel is an astonishingly appetizing delight.

2 tablespoons light extra virgin olive oil
¼ pound Shiitake mushrooms, julienned
¼ pound Portobello mushrooms, finely chopped
1 tablespoon minced garlic
1 tablespoon Italian spice
1 pound frozen leaf spinach, thawed
4 large shallots, sliced
3 tablespoons Worcestershire sauce
Squeeze of lemon
Salt and freshly ground pepper to taste
10 sheets phyllo pastry
½ cup butter, melted
1 pound Boursin cheese

- Sauté mushrooms in olive oil with spices.
- Add spinach and shallots and cook 1 minute. Set aside to cool.
- Blend in Worcestershire, lemon, salt and pepper.
- Working quickly with phyllo on a jelly roll pan, butter each of the 10 sheets separately, laying one on top of the other.
- About 2" from the end nearest you, start spreading the spinach mixture on pastry.
- Make an indentation in the spinach and fill it with Boursin.
- Roll pastry up like a tube. Bake at 350° for about 12 - 15 minutes or until phyllo is lightly browned.
- Spread Smoked Chipotle Coulis in bottom of serving plate and place strudel on top to serve.

SMOKED CHIPOTLE COULIS

2 large dried chipotle peppers
4 cups bottled marinara sauce

- In ¾ cup boiling water, rehydrate peppers for about 5 minutes.
- Drain, slice and add to marinara.
- Simmer 30 - 40 minutes. Purée and strain.

RAGIN' CAJUN RED BEANS AND RICE

From: Doxey's Market

YIELD:
Serves 6

NOTES:
The health conscious ingredients in this recipe reflect the concerns of owners Pam and Jim Doxey for our physical well-being.

2   cups dry red beans, soaked overnight
2   bay leaves
1   teaspoon dried thyme
1   strip Kombu (a sea vegetable which aids in the digestion of beans)
1   cup celery, diced
3   cloves garlic, minced
1/2 cup fresh parsley, minced
2   tablespoons Tamari (a wheat-free soy sauce)
1   tablespoon Cajun seasoning
    Cayenne pepper to suit personal taste
    Basmati rice
    Red onion, minced
    Red pepper, chopped
    Additional parsley

- Rinse beans very well. Place in pot and add twice as much water, bay leaves, thyme and Kombu. Simmer until soft.

- Add celery, garlic, parsley, Tamari and Cajun seasoning. Simmer about 30 minutes more.

- Serve over Basmati rice (which smells like popcorn when cooking) for an exciting change from regular rice.

- Minced red onion, chopped red pepper and additional minced parsley make a beautiful garnish.

ROBERT'S STUFFED POTATOES

From: Robert's Market

YIELD:
Serves 12

NOTES:
A true and trusted neighborhood market reminiscent of our childhood and renowned for "Mrs. Cross' and Billy's" fine food.

6   large baking potatoes
2   ounces butter
4   ounces sour cream
$^2/_3$ cup buttermilk
    Salt and white pepper to taste
    Shredded Cheddar cheese
    Bacon bits (optional)

- Bake potatoes, wrapped in aluminum foil, in 375° oven approximately 1 $^1/_2$ hours.

- Remove foil wrappers and cut potatoes in half lengthwise.

- Scoop out pulp while still warm and place in mixing bowl. Leave enough pulp in skins to form a boat.

- Mix all ingredients except cheese and bacon. Mash by hand with potato masher, leaving mixture somewhat chunky.

- Fill skins with potato mixture. Top with cheese and bacon.

- Bake at 350° approximately 25 - 30 minutes.

SWEET CORN CAKES

From: The Baja Grill

YIELD:
Serves 24

NOTES:
This Corn Cake is an essential mouth cooler when sampling The Baja Grill's endless selection of hot sauces.

$^1/_2$ cup shortening
1 cup unsalted butter
2 cups masa (Mexican corn meal)
12 tablespoons lukewarm water
40 ounces canned white corn
12 tablespoons cornmeal
1 cup granulated sugar
1 tablespoon baking powder
$^1/_2$ teaspoon salt
$^1/_2$ cup heavy cream

- Place the shortening and butter into a large mixing bowl and blend until creamy.

- Add masa and water and mix until just blended.

- Purée the white corn in a food processor until liquid with some texture still remaining.

- Add corn purée to masa mixture and set aside.

- In another bowl, place cornmeal, sugar, baking powder and salt and mix well.

- Stir in heavy cream, mixing thoroughly.

- Fold the cornmeal mixture into the masa mixture and blend well.

- Pour into a buttered 9" x 13" pan and cover with aluminum foil.

- Bake at 350° for 40 to 50 minutes or until the edges just begin to brown.

- Remove from pan 10 minutes after removing from oven to prevent sticking. Cut into 24 squares.

MARINATED MUSHROOM SALAD

From: The Pilot House

YIELD:

Serves 4

NOTES:

Its historic site and riverfront deck make a dining experience at The Pilot House seem like a well deserved vacation.

1   pound very fresh white mushrooms
$^1/_2$ to $^3/_4$ cup good quality light olive oil (not extra-virgin)
6   tablespoons fresh lemon juice, or more to taste
1   teaspoon fresh minced tarragon or dill, or more to taste
$^1/_4$ teaspoon salt
      Freshly ground pepper to taste

- Gently wipe mushrooms clean with paper towels.

- Mix remaining ingredients together in a glass or stainless steel bowl.

- Slice mushrooms thinly so marinade can permeate and flavor each slice.

- Toss mushrooms in marinade and allow to stand for 1 - 2 hours, then refrigerate.

- Serve on a bed of mixed baby greens and lettuces, garnish with peeled, seeded ripe tomato and julienne carrots.

- Vary the herbal flavor and acidity to taste.

MARINATED SHRIMP AND CRAB SALAD

From: Sarah Hedgpeth

YIELD:

Serves 12-15

NOTES:

To allow flavors to marry refrigerate overnight.

MARINADE:

1 ½ cups white wine vinegar
4 tablespoons lemon juice
4 tablespoons sugar
2 teaspoons lemon pepper
¾ cup olive oil
1 teaspoon dry mustard
1 teaspoon thyme
1 teaspoon basil
2 tablespoons parsley, chopped
Dash of hot pepper sauce

• Blend marinade ingredients in a bowl.

SALAD:

2 pounds large shrimp, cooked and peeled
1 pound choice lump crab meat
1 pound fresh mushrooms, sliced
1 sweet red pepper, julienned
1 (14 ounce) can hearts of palm, drained and sliced
1 can sliced water chestnuts, drained
½ pound fresh or frozen snow peas

• Pour marinade over salad and toss. Refrigerate overnight.

• Drain before serving on a bed of lettuce.

SURF PUPPIES

From: The Surf Club

YIELD:
36

NOTES:

A traditional southern beach club which has been transformed into a unique dining experience by chef Craig La Breche.

3	cups white corn meal
1/2	cup flour
3	tablespoons baking powder
1 1/2	teaspoons salt
	Pinch cayenne pepper
1 1/2	cups buttermilk
4	eggs
1	cup minced onion
2	cloves garlic, minced
	Oil for deep frying

- Combine first five dry ingredients.
- Mix together thoroughly the next four ingredients.
- Stir liquid ingredients into dry.
- Let batter rest 15 minutes.
- Fry by heaping tablespoons in hot oil to brown on all sides, about 3 minutes.

SEABOURN'S DARK CHOCOLATE MOUSSE

From: The Seabourn Cruise Line

YIELD:

Serves 6

NOTES:

Even in a twelve foot rowboat this is a rich dessert.

16 ounces heavy cream
1 egg
1 egg yolk
10 ounces dark sweetened chocolate, melted
1 teaspoon cognac

- Whip the cream and chill.
- In a double boiler whisk the egg and the egg yolk until stiff.
- Whisk in the chocolate.
- Carefully fold in $1/4$ of the whipped cream.
- Stir in the cognac.
- Fold in remaining whipping cream and chill.
- Garnish with raspberries or small mint leaves.

CREME BRULÉE

From: Scott Fisher

YIELD:
Serves 8

NOTES:
*Chef Scott Fisher is
a purist in the art
of French cooking.*

1 quart heavy cream
1 cup half and half
3 vanilla beans, split
1 ¼ cup sugar
16 large egg yolks

- In a large saucepan, combine heavy cream, half and half and vanilla beans.
- Heat over medium heat until scalding, but not boiling.
- Let rest, covered, for 10 minutes.
- In a separate bowl, whisk egg yolks and sugar together.
- Whisk in 1 cup of the heated cream mixture to the yolks. Mix thoroughly.
- Add the yolk and cream mixture to the remaining cream.
- Strain the mixture into a bowl and ladle into ovenproof pans.
- Place pans in a larger pan containing water (a water-bath or bain-marie) and place in 375° oven until custard is firm, about 40 minutes.

TOPPING:

1 cup granulated sugar
1 cup brown sugar

- Blend both sugars in food processor.
- Sprinkle on top of cooled custard, covering entire surface.
- Place directly under hot broiler for 30 seconds to 1 minute, or until top is brown and bubbling.
- Professional chefs use a propane torch to brown top. This is not advised for the home cook!

CASSATA CAKE

From: Roy's Riverboat Landing

YIELD:

Serves 8 -10

NOTES:

Chef W. Randolph Bowles' Cassata Cake reflects the unique and delicious sweets served at Roy's Riverboat Landing.

BASIC SPONGE CAKE:

1	cup cake flour
1/2	teaspoon salt
6	eggs, separated
1	cup extra-fine sugar
1	tablespoon lemon juice
1	lemon rind, grated

- Sift flour and salt together and set aside.
- Beat egg yolks until thick and lemony in color. Set aside.
- Beat egg whites until stiff but not dry.
- Fold in sugar, 2 tablespoons at a time, to egg whites.
- Add lemon juice, grated rind, and fold in yolks.
- Fold in flour mixture.
- Pour into a greased 9" x 5" pan.
- Bake at 350° for 30 - 35 minutes.
- Remove from pan and cool on rack.
- Divide cake lengthwise into 3 even strips.

FILLING:

1 $^1/_4$ pounds whipped ricotta cheese
$^1/_2$ pound confectioners' sugar
$^1/_8$ teaspoon cinnamon
$^1/_2$ teaspoon vanilla extract
$^1/_8$ pounds semi-sweet chocolate chips
$^1/_4$ ounce Frangelica liqueur
$^1/_4$ - $^1/_2$ ounce Grand Marnier liqueur

- Combine and mix all ingredients.
- Spread filling between cake layers.

ICING:

$^1/_2$ pound cream cheese, room temperature
Confectioners' sugar to taste
Semi-sweet chocolate chips for garnish

- Whip until smooth and sweeten as desired.
- Ice cake and garnish with chocolate chips.

PECAN RUM CAKES

From: The Surf Club

YIELD:
6 dozen

NOTES:
A perfect and delicious use for seasonal pecans.

2 ½ cups cake flour, sifted
1 ½ cups sugar
1 teaspoon salt
3 ½ teaspoons baking powder
½ cup softened butter, margarine, or shortening
1 ½ teaspoons vanilla
¾ cup milk
4 egg whites, room temperature
½ teaspoon rum extract
¼ cup rum

- Preheat oven to 350°.
- Sift flour, sugar, salt and baking powder into large bowl of mixer.
- Add butter, vanilla and milk. Beat on low until blended. Then beat on medium for 2 minutes, occasionally scraping sides of bowl with rubber spatula.
- Add unbeaten egg whites, rum extract and rum. Beat 2 minutes longer on medium speed.
- Pour batter into one 13" x 9" x 2" pan, or two 8" pans, greased, floured and lined with wax paper.
- Bake 35 - 40 minutes, or until surface springs back when gently pressed with finger tip. Let cool and prepare icing.
- Cut cake into 1 ½-inch squares. Pour generous teaspoon of rum on each cake square.
- Spread icing on all sides and roll in chopped fresh pecans.

PECAN ICING

½ cup butter
3 scant cups powdered sugar, sifted
Pinch salt
4 tablespoons milk
1 teaspoon vanilla
1 cup rum
1 cup fresh chopped pecans

- Cream butter and sugar with electric beater until fluffy. Add salt and stir in milk. Keep beating until very fluffy and add vanilla.

ESPRESSO & CHOCOLATE CHEESECAKE

From: Caffe Phoenix

YIELD:

Serves 10

NOTES:

This is a great dessert to cap off an evening and to complete The Cook's Canvas collection of recipes.

10 ounces chocolate cookies
8 tablespoons melted butter, cooled
4 tablespoons very strong espresso
24 ounces cream cheese at room temperature
1 cup sugar
3 eggs
1 tablespoon finely ground espresso coffee beans
6 ounces semisweet chocolate, melted with $1/4$ cup whipping cream

- Preheat oven to 400°.

- Grind cookies in food processor and slowly pour in 6 tablespoons melted butter.

- Press crumbs on bottom and 1 $1/2$ inches up sides of a 9" or 10" spring formpan.

- Wrap outside of pan with aluminum foil.

- Beat the cream cheese until smooth, add sugar and continue beating until mixture is light and fluffy.

- Add eggs, one at a time, beating well after each addition.

- Mix in espresso, 2 tablespoons melted butter and ground coffee.

- Pour half the cheese mixture into the lined cake pan.

- Drop 5 tablespoons melted chocolate in the filling and swirl with a sharp knife.

- Add remaining cheese mixture.

- Drop remaining chocolate in center 6 inches of cake and swirl.

- Bake cheesecake until edges are puffed and beginning to crack and top is golden brown (about 40 minutes). Center will not be set. Run knife around edge of pan to loosen. Release pan sides.

- Let stand at room temperature at least 30 minutes.

The Cook's Canvas Committee

Bebe Adams
Karen Albee
Nancy Alexander
Connie Anderson
Nancy Anderson
Sarah Anderson
Agnes Anthony
Debbie Austin
Dianne Avery
Bunnie Bachman
Pat Baker
Ede Baldridge
Carol Ballard
Rosalind Barker
Barbara Barre
Carole Battis
Carol Baumgariter
Judy Beam
Betsy Bede
Donald Bergstrom
Janie Bird
Ellen Birrell
Lelia Birrell
Ruby Bissette
Lillian Blakeman
Mary Blanken
Margie Bobbitt
Mary Bolin
Anne Bolles
Dorothy Bonitz
Judy Booth
Judy Bowman
Melissa Bowman
Karen Boyer
J. Bright
Kay Britto
Jane Broder
Louise Brooks
Betty Brown
Ruth Brown
Helen Brumbaugh
Ruth Brune
Tammala Bulger
David Bunn
Beachy Bunting
Jeane Burrows
Mary Will Burton
Caroline Butts

Betty Cameron
Hilda Cameron
Jill Carter
Rosa Champney
Jane Cipolla
Janis Clark
Barbara Coggeshall
Lynn Collins
Ann Combs
Gerrie Congdon
Helen Conrad
Marie Cooke
Betty Cooper
Bonnie Cooper
Mary Lou Corbin
Wanda Cornelius
Judy Cowan
Sharon Craig
Anne Craven
Ruth Crosby
Nancy Curry
Carol Davis
Paula Dayvault
Susan DeGroote
Gordie DePaolis
Paula DeSimone
Elizabeth Donald
Randi Duch
Peggy Duch
Lynn Dunlea
Pat Dunn
Hazel Efird
Bonnie Faler
Carol Farbolin
Gladys Faris
Alouise Fenstermacher
Robin Fernandez
Justine Ferrari
Kay Fife
Ann Finklestein-Adelman
Frances Fiorillo
Mike Fiorillo
Leslie Fleming
Debra Flora
Diana Foster
Ann Frederick
Bob Frederick
Judy Fulk

Ruth Funk
Betty Gaffney
DeLean Gardner
Doris Gardner
Dean Gatone
Marge Gerlach
Angela Gilbert
Hilda Godwin
Jean Goff
Vickie Goldenberg
Jane Goodhue
Pam Gordon
Jean Graham
Louise Graham
Esther Granfield
Marta Greene
Marty Gresham
Linda Grice
Ann Grose
Susan Habas
Robin Hackney
Lynn Haley
Berta Hamilton
Pat Hardison
Virginia Hardy
Darby Harris
Care Heeks
Stephanie Henrickson
Aggie Henriksen
Twila Hentz
Andrea Herring
Margee Herring
Frances Holdford
Angie Holliday
Barbara Hopper
Betty Hossfeld
Claude Howell
Becky Hughes
Josephine Huntt
Ellison Hunter
Melynda Hunter
Harriet Iiames
Penny Jackson
Elaine Johansen
Georgia Joyner
Joy Kalogeropoulos
Emeline Keith
Marie Kiely

Janis Kingoff
Sandra Kittinger
Rosemary Kline
Dee Langston
Geraldine LaVechi
Marilyn Lennard
Linda Lentz
Jean Lenzner
John Leonard
Julie Leviner
Jane Lewallen
Nancy Lierle
William Lloyd
Celeste Lofton
Happy Lowden
Janet K. Lowden
Lynn Lowder
Jinger Lyon
Edie Machado
Shirley MacKay
Lynn MacQueen
Louisa MacPherson
Hugh MacRae
Alberta Maher
Stephanie Mannen
Kay Marshburn
Jane Martin
Chris McArtor
Melanie McArtor
Betty McComas
Nilda McComas
Tabitha Hutaff McEachern
Gerald McKenzie
Paula McKenzie
Nancy McNaughton
John Millett
Joan Millette
Lore Millick
Jane Monroe
Margaret Moore
Phillip Morgan
Marianna Morrow
Nola Nadeau
M.A. Nelson
Glana Nichols
Donna Noyes
Melva O'Connor
Rosemary O'Hayer

Betty Oliver
Ruby Omirly
Loraine Oppenheimer
Anna C. Packard
Bette Page
Mary Jo Pappas
Joann Parker-Aikens
Mary Beth Parker
Vickie Parkinson
Bette Parrett
Sarah Parsley
Jan Paterson
Katherine Phillips
Nancy Phillips
Shay Pittillo
Ladeen Puddy
Bunny Rafferty
Georgia Reese
Phiney Rhinehart
Mary Lou Rhodes
Martie Rice
Mary Anne Rogers
Betsy Rollins
Mel Rollins
Lillian Romanak
Angela Romanek
Jean Rosenberg
Jan Rouse
Doris Ruffner
Elise Running
Betty Rusher
Joyce Russell
Babs Ryan
Despina Saffo
Janis Sass
Jinney Sceiford
Kay S. Schaal
Florence Schorschinsky
Millicent Sims
Hellen Slaice
Dixey Smith
Jim Smith
Julie Smith
Mildred Smith
Kelly Smith-Petricola
Alicia Sneeden
Edith Sneeden
Joyce Southerland

Mrs. Mickey Southerland
Kenneth Sprunt
Anne Squire
Margaret Stanback
Sherry Stokely
Minnie Stone
Jocelyn Strange
Jane Sullivan
Katherine Sullivan
Scott Sullivan
Mrs. William Sutton
Gretter Talbert
Diane Talley
Suzanne Taylor
Joan Thompson
Nancy Thompson
Betty Tinsley
Marcy Tonkinson
Frankie Trask
Ann Turlington
Lisa Turner
Christa Walker
Jean Walthal
Dorothy Wango
Allison Ward
Robin Ward
Faith Waters
Ann Watkins
Ruth Webb
Dottie Werk
Emile Werk
Lillie White
Michelle White
Polly White
Mimi Whitford
Freda Wilkins
Marianna Williams
Avery Wilmeth
Gloria Woodell
Mrs. Jerry Woodell
Anne Woodworth
Mrs. F.R.W. Worth
Rushie Wrenn-Collins
Elizabeth Wright
Maureen Ywaskevic
Ronna Zimmer
Roberta Zimmer

The Cook's Canvas
St. John's Museum of Art
114 Orange Street, Wilmington, NC 28401
910-763-7556 Telephone
910-341-7981 FAX

Please send me _____ copies of

      The Cook's Canvas at $24.95 each _____

    North Carolina residents add $1.50 each _____

Please gift wrap _____ copies at $3.00 each _____

    Plus postage and handling of $3.00 per copy _____

                  Total _____

Enclosed is a check for $ _____ .
Payable to: St. John's Museum of Art.

I prefer to pay by credit card: _____ VISA _____ MasterCard

Account number _____ Exp. Date _____

Cardholder's signature _____

Name _____

Address _____

City _____ State _____ Zip _____

Telephone _____

Mailing Label

Name _____

Address _____

City _____

State _____ Zip _____

Gift from: _____

Mailing Label

Name _____

Address _____

City _____

State _____ Zip _____

Gift from: _____

- -

The Cook's Canvas
St. John's Museum of Art
114 Orange Street, Wilmington, NC 28401
910-763-7556 Telephone
910-341-7981 FAX

Please send me _____ copies of

      The Cook's Canvas at $24.95 each _____

    North Carolina residents add $1.50 each _____

Please gift wrap _____ copies at $3.00 each _____

    Plus postage and handling of $3.00 per copy _____

                  Total _____

Enclosed is a check for $ _____ .
Payable to: St. John's Museum of Art.

I prefer to pay by credit card: _____ VISA _____ MasterCard

Account number _____ Exp. Date _____

Cardholder's signature _____

Name _____

Address _____

City _____ State _____ Zip _____

Telephone _____

Mailing Label

Name _____

Address _____

City _____

State _____ Zip _____

Gift from: _____

Mailing Label

Name _____

Address _____

City _____

State _____ Zip _____

Gift from: _____

The Cook's Canvas
St. John's Museum of Art
114 Orange Street, Wilmington, NC 28401
910-763-7556 Telephone
910-341-7981 FAX

ease send me _____ copies of
    The Cook's Canvas at $24.95 each _____

    North Carolina residents add $1.50 each _____

ease gift wrap _____ copies at $3.00 each _____

    Plus postage and handling of $3.00 per copy _____

                                Total _____

nclosed is a check for $ _____ .
ayable to: St. John's Museum of Art.

prefer to pay by credit card: _____ VISA _____ MasterCard

ccount number _____ Exp. Date _____

ardholder's signature _____

ame _____

ddress _____

ity _____ State _____ Zip _____

elephone _____

Mailing Label

Name _____

Address _____

City _____

State _____ Zip _____

Gift from: _____

Mailing Label

Name _____

Address _____

City _____

State _____ Zip _____

Gift from: _____

- -

The Cook's Canvas
St. John's Museum of Art
114 Orange Street, Wilmington, NC 28401
910-763-7556 Telephone
910-341-7981 FAX

ease send me _____ copies of
    The Cook's Canvas at $24.95 each _____

    North Carolina residents add $1.50 each _____

ease gift wrap _____ copies at $3.00 each _____

    Plus postage and handling of $3.00 per copy _____

                                Total _____

nclosed is a check for $ _____ .
ayable to: St. John's Museum of Art.

prefer to pay by credit card: _____ VISA _____ MasterCard

ccount number _____ Exp. Date _____

ardholder's signature _____

ame _____

ddress _____

ity _____ State _____ Zip _____

elephone _____

Mailing Label

Name _____

Address _____

City _____

State _____ Zip _____

Gift from: _____

Mailing Label

Name _____

Address _____

City _____

State _____ Zip _____

Gift from: _____